ELIJAH AND ELISHA

ELIJAH AND ELISHA

Expositions from the Book of Kings

RONALD S. WALLACE

WIPF & STOCK · Eugene, Oregon

Wipf and Stock Publishers
199 W 8th Ave, Suite 3
Eugene, OR 97401

Elijah and Elisha
Expositions from the Book of Kings
By Wallace, Ronald
ISBN 13: 978-1-62032-833-0
Publication date 1/15/2013
Previously published by Wm. B. Eerdmans, 1957

To

David and Elizabeth and Heather

PREFACE

THIS IS A SERIES of expositions of most of the passages in the first and second books of Kings which give the history of the two prophets, Elijah and Elisha. Some of these stories are among the most vivid and memorable in the Old Testament, and have never failed to prove themselves relevant and challenging in the preaching of the Church. Others of them present what to many are the most difficult moral and intellectual problems both for the preacher and the listener.

I have treated these stories as having a living and real basis in the historical life of the people of God. Yet I have tried to expound them so that those who cannot accept them as historical might at least become instructed by what they teach even when they are regarded merely as stories. I have not consciously followed any rigid rules of interpretation, but I have tried to avoid exaggerated allegorical interpretations especially where the passage, viewed historically, had another obvious meaning.

Each of us can profit from the Scripture only according to our faith. Some will have no difficulty in accepting as history what to others can only remain mere story. Some will be able to find inspiration and instruction and profit in an allegorical interpretation which others will reject. In this matter the expositor will be guided by the attitude of the congregation to whom he is preaching, and these studies have all been preached. No preacher can avoid giving offence to some, if his preaching is Biblical. Yet the preacher must seek not to offend where the Gospel does not necessarily offend.

We need not assume, however, that the listeners in the average congregation today are so biased against the difficult miracle stories of the Old Testament that they will refuse to allow themselves to be taught from them. People will begin to find themselves more able to accept the events of the Bible as historical if they are constantly challenged by the meaning of these events in the context of their proclamation within the worship and fellowship of the Church.

FOREWORD

BY THE REV. PROFESSOR JAMES BARR
NEW COLLEGE, EDINBURGH

THE USE OF THE Old Testament in Christian preaching is being widely discussed at present, most actively of all perhaps on the European continent. Scholars of no less importance in the historical-critical field than Noth or von Rad have participated in this discussion. The systematic theologian, van Ruler of Utrecht, has devoted a provocative monograph to it. Typological and allegorical methods of interpretation have enjoyed a certain revival. Meanwhile the Church in certain tragic situations has found to its surprise how the Old Testament can come alive to the worshipping community.

Nevertheless a widespread uncertainty remains in the minds of scholars, clergy and laity alike. Certain sonorous texts and certain sublime passages of the Old Testament have never failed to gain attention from the pulpit. Other passages have seemed "difficult", and it has seemed uncertain whether they carried a message at all, or whether if such could be found it would be reconcilable with the main insights of the Christian faith. In these circumstances the preacher is tempted to neglect intractable material rather than wrestle with it. Mr. Wallace here takes the tradition of Elijah and Elisha and attempts an exposition of the material as a whole, and not of one or two choice sentences within it. If the understanding and appropriation of the Old Testament is to be revived within the Church, it can only be by this attention to and exposition of the traditions as a whole.

Mr. Wallace writes as a practical preacher and theologian. The critical sciences of Old Testament study are without the scope of these sermons, and modern historical and philological research is sparingly used. Their significance is in the realm of Christian hermeneutics. The writer has nowhere codified his principles of interpretation. But two points at least can be discerned. Firstly, the reality of the God who spoke to and acted through Elijah and Elisha. Mr. Wallace sees the Christian as committed not only to the God of Peter and John but to the God of Elijah and Elisha. He is not, however, equally committed to the full correctness of every action or conception of these men. Secondly, he interprets the events for the most part analogically. Analogy is quite different from allegory, which reads into a text a secret meaning in terms of an alien system, and from typology, which sees a hidden special correspondence with an antitype. Analogy means a likeness of pattern in God's act and men's response at various times, but not an identity of content or situation.

These sermons should be a real stimulus to all who believe that the Old Testament has an essential place in Christian preaching.

CONTENTS

	PAGE
The Word of the living God	1
Cherith and Zarephath	10
Elijah and the Widow woman	18
Searchlight on the hidden Church	25
Decision at Mount Carmel	33
Elijah's flight	43
The call of Elisha	54
Naboth's vineyard	62
Ahaziah and Elijah	71
Elisha succeeds to his task	79
At Jericho and Bethel	89
In the home of the Widow	97
The Shunammite	107
Three Miracles	118
Naaman	127
Syria wars against Israel	140
The siege of Samaria	147
The death of Elisha	156

THE WORD OF THE LIVING GOD

And Elijah the Tishbite, who was of the inhabitants of Gilead, said unto Ahab, As the Lord God of Israel liveth, before whom I stand, there shall not be dew nor rain these years, but according to my word.

I KINGS 17.1

ISRAEL

In the reign of Ahab and Jezebel a critical religious and political situation arose in the land of Israel. In marrying Jezebel, the princess of Tyre, Ahab, king of Israel, had chosen a woman of a religion utterly different from his own. No doubt he expected her to give up her religion for his when she came to Israel, but instead of this Jezebel made Ahab mix his own religion with an overwhelming proportion of hers. She brought with her from Tyre not only her dowry but also an army of hundreds of priests of the religion of Baal, and she set up altars to Baal in palace and temple.

Her arrival therefore made Baal worship alarmingly popular in Israel. It had indeed already been going on in the land for years before Jezebel appeared on the scene. Many Israelites had already bowed the knee to Baal unobtrusively and in a way that did not outwardly conflict with their worship of the Lord God, but after Jezebel's arrival, instead of being a hidden superstition, the religion of Baal became an openly avowed and militant force threatening the whole religion and moral tradition of Israel. Baal became a rival god to the Lord Himself. Jezebel's priests began to teach the young in Israel to call upon the name of Baal as their fathers had been taught to call upon the name of the Lord.

They taught the people that Baal had been the true god of Canaan long before Israel had set foot in the land to bring in the new foreign religion of Abraham and Moses. They taught that Baal was still powerful to bless them, and could give them fertility in their fields and homes. The Lord was indeed a great God who had brought them out of the land of Egypt. He was the God of their history and of their past. But Baal also had a great deal to do with their everyday life. He was the god who filled their cradles and their sheepfolds and their cattlesheds with young. Baal could control the rain and give them good crops. When they heard this teaching the mass of the people of Israel took it seriously. Though they did not want to forsake the religion of the Lord, they felt it would be a good thing to keep on the right side of Baal.

A political and religious crisis was bound to come. In her determination to spread the religion of Baal Jezebel took ruthless political action. She came from a country where rule was despotic and where to be a queen meant to be a tyrant. Her method of breaking down opposition was either to murder or to force into hiding the priests of the Lord who dared to resist the change in the religion of their land.

But there was not at first much resistance. Few seemed to care very much about the preservation either of liberty or of truth. Even though their freedom was being threatened as well as their religion, most people showed no sign of alarm. Trade was good. Money was flowing into their country from Tyre, the land of Baal. Goods were cheap and plentiful. They felt they had economic security. There was no unemployment. What did it matter to the people if their government showed sinister tendencies towards totalitarianism? What did it matter to them that Ahab and Jezebel occasionally put on the air of tyrants and spoke untraditionally? What did it matter to adhere strictly to the religious traditions of their fathers? They were willing to keep Ahab and Jezebel in power as long as bread and corn were plentiful and wine was flowing cheaply. Such was the situation that Elijah had to face.

Today again we live in an age when dictators are only too ready to make their appearance on the political scene, and it is well that we should allow ourselves to be reminded in these chapters of the Bible that what God gives to a nation in one generation can be very quickly forfeited by succeeding generations if they do not value fully their heritage of liberty, or if they compromise with evil.

The Living God

As soon as Jezebel appeared in control of government in Israel there also appeared a man of God whose task was to witness to the living God and to set in motion the forces of resistance that would ultimately overthrow Ahab and Jezebel. '*And Elijah the Tishbite, who was of the inhabitants of Gilead, said unto Ahab, As the Lord God of Israel liveth, before whom I stand, there shall not be dew nor rain these years, but according to my word.*' Elijah appears on the scene with startling suddenness. Indeed, his appearance is a mystery. We want to know more about this man when we suddenly see him stand before the king. We want to know where he came from, and where he was trained in the things of God. We want to know how he received his call to be a prophet to his time. But we know as little about him as Ahab knew about him, and it is better so. For to see him appear thus reminds us that we need not despair when we see great movements of evil achieving spectacular success on this earth, for we may be sure that God, in unexpected places, has already secretly prepared His countermovement. God has always His ways of working underground to undermine the stability of evil. God can raise men for His service from nowhere. He can use 'things which are not, to bring to nought things that are'.[1] Therefore the situation is never hopeless where God is concerned. Whenever evil flourishes, it is always a superficial flourish, for at the height of the triumph of evil God will be there, ready with His man and His movement and His plans to ensure that His own cause will never fail.

'*The Lord God of Israel liveth*,' Elijah cried. This was the burden of his whole ministry: 'The Lord who will not tolerate evil, the jealous God who will not allow His name to be tied up with any other name, still lives! Events are to take place in Israel that will prove He is still mighty! Judgment is coming to prove to men the bitterness of forsaking God! *The Lord God of Israel liveth!*'

It had not occurred to Ahab that the Lord God of his fathers still lived! He and Jezebel in planning their kingdom had confidently assumed that the Lord was dead. They had

[1] 1 Cor. 1.28

thought that the old ideas of a God who would have no compromise with other gods were all exploded. They had imagined therefore that the religion of the Lord could be easily altered to suit the spirit and moods of each generation. They had thought that the teaching of Moses was outmoded, and that true progress required the continual sacrifice of dead gods and the setting up of altars to new ones in each generation.

Moreover, even the faithful believers in the Lord who still remained in the land of Israel were wondering if the Lord was indeed alive after all. If He was a living God, what was He doing? Why was He so calm and indifferent? Did He not see the temples reared up to Baal in this land which was supposed to be His own peculiar possession? Did He not hear the blasphemy that was being poured out of the lips of His own people, young and old, as they responded to the call to invoke Baal in their temples, and to take Baal alongside the Lord in their affections? Elijah brought them the victorious and assuring answer: '*The Lord God of Israel liveth!*' He has seen and He has heard, and He still lives to fulfil His righteousness!

Moreover, the living God had not only seen and heard, but He was about to act in judgment. He had been slow to act. In His longsuffering He had waited until Ahab and Jezebel should repent. But Ahab and Jezebel had assumed that His longsuffering was merely a sign that there was no living God. Ahab is described in the Scriptures as 'provoking the Lord to anger'[1] by flouting His mercy and goodness. God's anger can be provoked. Though God gives man a long time and allows him to go far in wickedness before He is provoked to anger, nevertheless ultimately He acts with startling suddenness and firm purpose. He brought punishment in Israel. He visited the land with famine. No rain fell for three years.

In this judgment God punished not only the king but also the people. In the sight of God people and rulers are closely bound up together, and the people are regarded as being responsible for their government. When people who have been bred in freedom yield to tyrants they displease God. Israel, as a nation, is regarded as guilty for encouraging and tolerating Ahab. In this fearful judgment that came upon king and people, those whose indifference to politics had helped to bring

[1] 1 Kings 16.33

about the tragedy in Israel suffered no less than those who had been active in their wickedness.

In the midst of His judgment upon Israel God made sure that everyone would know what He was doing. When He sent the famine, He sent a man to interpret what the famine meant. He spoke a word through Elijah that left the people in no doubt that it was their God who had done this thing. Otherwise, the people of Israel might still have accepted the famine, and yet evaded the challenge of God to repent. They might have explained the famine by putting it down to evil spirits. They might have concocted some primitive scientific explanation for the lack of rainfall. They might have said, 'Baal has fallen asleep'. But with the memory of Elijah standing there before them, promising this terrible punishment in the name of God, they knew when the famine came that there was only one explanation, one meaning in this disaster. It was a judgment and a call from the Lord. They must repent, for the Lord God of Israel was still the living God! The famine was a sign to them that the Lord was stronger than Baal, and that it was the Lord and not Baal who controlled the weather and gave them fruitfulness.

THE MAN OF GOD

Undoubtedly in many ways Elijah was a man fitted for his task. The situation in Israel required a man of courage and determination to speak out his convictions. Elijah was such a man. The times needed a man whose character was as strong as Jezebel's, and who could inspire in Ahab as much fear as she did. Elijah had the makings of such a man. He was a man of action, for drastic action was to be demanded of him. He was not an original thinker, for his task was to recall the nation to faithfulness to its past. Therefore he was in many respects like the great men of Israel's past history. He was like Moses. He made the men of his day uncomfortable by reminding them of the God of their fathers whom they had forsaken, and by acting so that men felt that he was indeed a prophet of the Lord.

God knows the type of man required for each situation in life and God seeks to match His men with the task that is to be done. It is true that however many or great may be our gifts and talents we are always hopelessly inadequate for the work God wants us to do. Nevertheless He will not send us forth to any task without giving us the gifts we require and making us in some measure fitted, even on a human level, to face the challenge of our surroundings. 'The times were fit for Elijah,' writes Bishop Hall, 'and Elijah was fit for them. The eminentest prophet is reserved for the corruptest age. Israel never had such a king for impiety; nor so miraculous a prophet as Elijah. . . . The God of spirits knows how to apportion men for the occasion.'

But what holds our attention above everything else as we watch Elijah in action is his serene consciousness of being chosen by God to act as intermediary between God and Israel. He claims to have been placed in a position of unquestionable authority to speak for God to his times. 'I stand before God,' he cries to his generation. He claims to be able to speak in the name and in the place of God. He speaks with serene confidence that what he says indeed truly represents God's attitude. He claims to be able truly to interpret and announce God's will for His people.

Moreover, he stands before God not only to speak God's Word to Israel but also to pray for Israel to God. In a sense Elijah represented Israel to God, as well as God to Israel. We catch glimpses of him praying to God for Israel and suffering before God for the people he represented. To Elijah it became such a heavy burden of responsibility to stand between God and Israel that at times he wanted to flee from his task and resign the burden altogether.

In all this we are reminded of Jesus Christ. He is the one true Mediator between God and man. None of us can stand directly before God to hear what God has to say to us, but Jesus is the One who stands before God for us for ever. Therefore we can come to Him to hear the true and never-failing Word of God for our needs. Elijah at times misrepresented and misinterpreted God. He was sometimes mistaken in the word he uttered in the name of God. But Jesus always perfectly interpreted God to man. That is why the New Testament speaks of Him as the One who comes forth from the bosom of the Father, or as the One in whose face we see the glory of God Himself.

Jesus also stands before God to pray for us and to offer Himself for us. We dare not try to offer ourselves as we are to God, for we are sinners. But Jesus can stand in our place before God. There He can offer Himself for us, and can ask God to accept us for His sake. That is why God accepts us. Jesus always perfectly represents us to God. He is the One in whom there is no sin, the One who pleased the Father perfectly.

Elijah, as we shall see, could only partially fulfil the task of witnessing to God in his generation, and because of his frailty his life and influence were the less effective. But Jesus Christ was and is ever the true man of God in whom we can perfectly trust and in whom God perfectly trusts. Therefore His Kingdom and influence and intercession shall never fail.

THE WORD OF POWER

When Elijah spoke his word, God spoke by miracle. '*There shall not be dew nor rain these years, but according to my word,*' cried Elijah, and it happened. The Bible shows us a God who speaks in the language that men understand. The men of these times understood the language of miracles, therefore God spoke such a language. They understood what was meant by national catastrophe and famine, and God spoke to them in such language. When Elijah under his burning conviction of the nearness of God said, '*There shall not be dew nor rain,*' there was drought in the land. When Elijah challenged the Lord God to send fire from Heaven to witness for His cause before the people, God spoke by fire from Heaven. It is true that Elijah was a man of few words. We have no 'Book oi Elijah' in the Bible, and no account of long sermons preached by him. But what words he spoke were effective to bring to pass what they commanded or promised because they were indeed the Word of God. It would be difficult otherwise to explain the effectiveness of Elijah's influence as a prophet and the change he brought about in the history of Israel.

It is still true that God must speak by miracle today if His Word is to be effective within the Church. We are greatly concerned over the seeming irrelevance and impotence of much of our modern preaching. The Word we proclaim does not seem to go home to create burning conviction within men's hearts, and we ourselves find it hard to feel that behind our words there is indeed the full authority of the Lord God. God does not seem to speak as we speak in His name. Some people call this problem 'the problem of communication', and they urge us to rethink our whole attempt to communicate divine power and divine truth to this modern generation. They tell us that we need a new technique. We must simplify our language. We must study more carefully the mind of the men to whom we are preaching. Such criticism of the way we preach may be justified and such a rethinking of our methods may be required. Nevertheless we must remember that if our words are to be effective we too require that God should speak by miracle as we speak in His name. We certainly do not require that God should witness to the truth of His Word by enabling it to effect such spectacular wonders as are recorded in the Old Testament to have taken place before the eyes of men. God has already witnessed to the truth of the Word we preach in Jesus Christ crucified and risen from the dead. Whereas an Elijah needed signs and wonders to witness to the truth of his word, we have the living Christ present with us. We have the Holy Spirit powerful within the life of the Church. We have the whole Bible. Yet preaching even today cannot be effective unless God gives His witness along with the Word. The miracle therefore for which we wait as we stand before the world to speak in the name of God is simply the miracle of the coming of the Holy Ghost to make manifest in the midst of the Church that Jesus Christ is risen from the dead, all-powerful to work His miracles of grace and healing in the souls of men, and all-powerful to bring in the day when the whole material realm will be changed and His Kingdom will finally come.

There is nothing we need more today in our preaching in the Church than the same conviction as burned within Elijah's heart as he spoke to his generation. We need the conviction that we indeed stand before God and that our word has therefore His authority and His power to judge those to whom it is proclaimed, to bring them to the hour of decision and to convey to our hearers the very grace it promises.

Elijah got no support from anyone on that day when he stood before the public and announced the Word of the Lord.

He had to go away into hiding until the economic condition of the country had changed, and the crisis of which he was warning the people was actually upon them. It was only after Israel had experienced three years of famine that men became convinced that even economically totalitarianism did not work when there was a God in Heaven, and God was against it. Then after three terrible years of famine Elijah reappeared. His public career was brief. He brought about one whirlwind revolution, but what he did so deeply impressed itself on the minds of the people that the consequences were lasting. Elijah completely destroyed confidence in the ruling house of Omri. He saved the cause of true religion in his day, and made it possible for a generation of prophets to arise after him to continue to witness with boldness and conviction to the Lord God of Israel.

CHERITH AND ZAREPHATH

And the word of the Lord came unto him, saying, Get thee hence, and turn thee eastward, and hide thyself by the brook Cherith, that is before Jordan. And it shall be, that thou shalt drink of the brook; and I have commanded the ravens to feed thee there. So he went and did according unto the word of the Lord: for he went and dwelt by the brook Cherith, that is before Jordan. And the ravens brought him bread and flesh in the morning, and bread and flesh in the evening; and he drank of the brook. And it came to pass after a while, that the brook dried up, because there had been no rain in the land. And the word of the Lord came unto him, saying, Arise, get thee to Zarephath, which belongeth to Zidon, and dwell there: behold I have commanded a widow woman there to sustain thee.

I KINGS 17.2-9

'HIDE THYSELF'

Immediately after he had begun his ministry and had announced so dramatically that God's judgment on Israel was to be three years of famine, Elijah was told by God to go into retreat. '*Get thee hence, and turn thee eastward, and hide thyself by the brook Cherith.*'

On first thoughts we wonder why Elijah should be told by God to hide himself. We find it hard to understand this command, for from one point of view it does not seem very brave or noble conduct on Elijah's part to pronounce judgment and then flee. It looks as if he wanted to avoid the effects of the Word he proclaimed. It does not seem consistent conduct for him to appear so boldly and interfere with such a devastating word in the politics and religion of his time, and then, having upset everybody and everything, to go away into hiding and try to live a quiet life.

Nevertheless, when we think it all over in the light of what is to follow, we can see real meaning and purpose in God's call to Elijah to hide himself, and as we follow him into the desert to Cherith and watch him there we can learn with him one or two important lessons.

At Cherith Elijah was protected with complete security

from the enemies who were hunting him throughout the length and breadth of the land. He was fed by ravens as if from Heaven while famine raged all round. He was refreshed by the water of the brook while drought prevailed everywhere else. To be hidden and sustained in this way, even though it may have been only for a short period, was for Elijah the kind of sign he needed from God at this time in his life. God, by calling him to be His prophet, had thrust Elijah out into public life and had made him a target for the intense hatred of Jezebel and Ahab and multitudes of starving people who in the wilderness of their grief would no doubt blame him for their sorry plight. God was going to send him forth again to stand alone in conflict with the whole world of his time. Elijah's experience at Cherith lasted long enough to teach him in a most concrete way a lesson he must never forget. Whatever his future circumstances might be, he could now be assured that he would enjoy the protection of the Lord. In the ultimate issue of things he would know that he did not depend upon man, and he would be upheld and sustained by his relation to God Himself.

The experience in our own lives that corresponds most readily to that of Elijah at the brook Cherith is, of course, our experience at the Lord's Table. Life may not be so turbulent for us as it was for Elijah; nevertheless it is disturbing enough to make us feel our need for some concrete evidence of God's love and care for us as individuals. When we come apart from the world to celebrate the Lord's Supper God gives to us a sign no less wonderful and no less assuring than that which he gave to Elijah by means of the ravens at the brook Cherith. The Lord's Supper is a sign of God's love and care given to us in the midst of this world in which there appear so many signs of God's judgment. It is a sign that in the midst of temptation and persecution we can draw our protection from Him. At the Lord's Supper it is proclaimed to us by means of the symbols of bread and wine given to us in complete seclusion from the world that our true life is hid with Christ in God.[1] There, moreover, the life and strength that are ours in Jesus Christ are actually given to us as we eat and drink at the Table which God has prepared. At the Lord's Table Christ

[1] Col. 3.3

says to us precisely what He sought to say to His servant Elijah at the brook Cherith. 'Peace I leave with you, my peace I give unto you: not as the world giveth, give I unto you. Let not your heart be troubled, neither let it be afraid.'[1] At the Lord's Table He seeks to make us lift up our hearts to the things that are above in order to remind us that we belong not only to this present world but also to that world which is to come.

Therefore perhaps the Word '*Hide thyself*' is spoken by God to us as well as to Elijah. In several places in the Gospels we are shown Jesus Himself deliberately withdrawing and hiding from the crowds. On one occasion, when He saw that His disciples were becoming too immersed in work and too harassed and troubled in spirit, He said to them, 'Come ye yourselves apart into a desert place, and rest a while.'[2] If we learned to hide ourselves more from the world we are seeking to serve in the name of Christ, we might gain the extra courage and strength we need to serve it more efficiently and more effectively. If we became more separate from the world in spirit, we might be able more clearly to understand God's Word for His world, and more bold and courageous in proclaiming with word and life the whole counsel of God for our time.

'GET THEE TO ZAREPHATH'

Elijah was not allowed to stay indefinitely at Cherith enjoying the luxury of sheltered seclusion from the troubles of earth. It would have been bad for his soul to have left him there too long, for he was not by nature a sociable man and the solitude and quietness of Cherith would have exactly suited his tastes. In any case, this was surely no time for a man of God to isolate himself too completely in solitary mystical devotion.

The word soon came to Elijah: '*Arise, get thee to Zarephath.*' In the cities and villages of Israel men and women and children were being deprived of food and water. Out in the fields in their misery and anxiety they were toiling away, scraping the hard earth for what little sustenance it would yield. The man who would be fit to preach the Word of God to His

---

[1] John. 14.27   [2] Mark 6.31

people must be as far as he can a pastor and friend to those to whom he preaches the Word. He must have living, intimate contact with the sufferings and feelings and problems of those to whom he has been sent by God to minister. Elijah the preacher must not try to divorce himself from all this. So God said, 'Arise, Elijah, you have had enough of this seclusion, and enough of this sheltered privilege, before me! Arise and get back to human life! Arise, you preacher of the Word, and regain contact with those whose existence has been so bitterly affected by the Word you have spoken in my name! *Arise, get thee to Zarephath!*' Elijah belonged to Israel and Israel was suffering. Why should the prophet of God be exempt from the temptations and hardships of the people to whom he was to minister the things of God?

In the book of Ezekiel there is a passage where the prophet describes how he had a vision of God's glory when he was caught up to Heaven by the Spirit to hear the Word of judgment he was to preach to Israel. In this vision he was warned about how this Word would create antagonism between himself and those to whom he preached. Nevertheless, immediately after the vision Ezekiel was sent back to Tel-abib amongst the very people to whom he was to minister the Word of judgment, 'and,' he writes, 'I sat where they sat, and remained there astonished among them seven days.'[1] A prophet must allow himself not only to be caught up by the Spirit to Heaven, but must also mix with those to whom he is to preach, stand alongside them, sit with them, suffer with them. Elijah, too, at Cherith began to understand that if he wanted to stand before God as His prophet to Israel, he had to sit among God's people even while they suffered under His judgment. He must now enter the life of a humble home in Israel. He must come to understand with real depth of feeling the fears and sorrows of a poor widow woman, one of the multitude who were suffering because of the Word of judgment he had preached.

It is when we think of Jesus Christ that we understand why the bearer of the Word of God must sit among the people to whom he preaches. For Jesus was the One who stood nearer to God than any other man has ever done. He proclaimed

[1] Ezek. 3.15

His Word unerringly and without compromise. Yet He also sat among men and bore their sufferings and sorrows as no other prophet ever did. He was born of a woman, grew up in the midst of a typical humble home in Israel, learned by His experience of the things which He suffered. He endured hunger, thirst, weariness and disappointment. He indeed sat in our place, suffered in our place. He 'was in all points tempted like as we are'.[1] 'Himself took our infirmities, and bore our sicknesses.'[2] And in the end He so identified Himself with us that He stood where all of us should stand, but where none of us could bear to stand, under the full force of the judgment for sin that His Word so fearlessly and unerringly warned us about.

Cherith and Zarephath in the Christian Life

The New Testament is constantly reminding us that if we believe in Christ we belong at one and the same time to two different worlds and two different ages.

Because Jesus Christ has ascended above and beyond this world, and we have ascended in Him, we belong to the world that is above and the age that is to come. 'Our citizenship is in Heaven; from whence also we wait for a Saviour.'[3] Therefore in our relationship to this present world we can reflect the attitude symbolised by Elijah's lonely and secluded sojourn at Cherith. We must become separate in spirit and detached in heart and mind from this present world. We must constantly listen to the Word which tells us to seek those things which are above,[4] to abhor that which is evil,[5] and to have no fellowship with the unfruitful works of darkness.[6]

But because Jesus Christ came into this world in His Incarnation, and died on the Cross to save it, none of us dares deny that we belong also to this present world with its mass of individual and communal suffering, and its intricate maze of political and industrial problems. Therefore we must also reflect in our Christian life the attitude to this world symbolised by Elijah's stay at Zarephath. We must allow ourselves to become really involved in responsibility and care for all the crying problems around us. Even when we kneel

---

[1] Heb. 4.15 [2] Matt. 8.17 [3] Phil. 3.20 (R.V.)
[4] Col. 3.1 [5] Rom. 12.9 [6] Eph. 5.11

alone in prayer or gather at our Church worship we must constantly listen to the Word of God as it calls us back to life. For Jesus Christ by His Incarnation has bound us afresh to our neighbour through the ties of human flesh and blood which He Himself has again made common to both of us. The New Testament reminds us too that since Satan has been cast out of Heaven, if we want to be good soldiers of Jesus Christ the place where we are most likely to engage the enemy in concrete form is not Heaven but this present earth.[1]

Both Cherith and Zarephath, then, are represented in the life of the Christian man. Jesus called the twelve 'that *they should be with him*, and that He might *send them forth*'.[2] Jesus once said, 'I am the door: by me if any man enter in, he shall be saved, and *shall go in and out*, and find pasture'.[3] A Christian is a man who 'goes in and out', moving between two worlds, participating in the life of two different ages or realms. He has a very decided relationship, and a responsibility both towards what is beyond this world and towards what is in this world. This does not mean that he is a 'half and half' person, only half in Heaven and half on earth, only half-hearted in his 'otherworldliness' and half-hearted in his pursuit of his earthly calling and earthly duty. The fact that the Apostle Paul wanted to depart from this earth and be with Christ, which he said was 'far better',[4] did not make him any less prudent or practical or interested in earthly things than the man who knows only one world. A Christian's wholehearted seeking after what is beyond does not make him unpractical or unloving. He can press towards the heavenly mark with full and concentrated energy and yet at the same time be wholehearted in his enjoyment of what his conscience and God's Word allow him to enjoy in earthly pleasure and in the service of his fellow men. Like Peter and James and John he will be able to ascend with Jesus up the Mount of Transfiguration and will become so fascinated and held by what is transcendent and otherworldly in the mystery of Jesus Christ that he will want to remain almost too long up there. But then he will follow Jesus Christ back down the mountain, right into the midst of the antagonism and need of the world which are so urgent and pressing that he has to forget for a moment

[1] Rev. 12.7-12   [2] Mark 3.14   [3] John 10.9   [4] Phil. 1.23

what happened up there in order to be able to give the love and attention that alone can meet the human situation.[1]

THE SIGN OF THE EMPTY BROOK

A sign was given to Elijah that it was time he went back to life: '*It came to pass after a while, that the brook dried up,*' and a promise was given along with the word that commanded him back to life: '*I have commanded a widow woman there to sustain thee.*'

This may surely be interpreted as if it were an allegory. We have to seek the things which are above. But whenever we seek to concentrate too much of our attention or to spend too large a proportion of our time in cultivating the 'devotional life' at the expense of our active Christian witness, then the heavenly brooks at which we seek to refresh ourselves and repair our spirits have a way of drying up. The bread by which our souls live must come down from Heaven, but whenever we seek to hide ourselves from the world too long and too completely in order to feed ourselves on this bread from Heaven, we will become more starved of it than ever in spite of all our praying and Bible-reading and churchgoing. The devotional life becomes unreal and unsatisfying when its 'cultivation' is made an end in itself or a selfish spiritual luxury. It becomes meaningful and vital only when it is kept as one aspect of a life that is as much involved and immersed in human activity as were those of all the great figures of the Bible.

Moreover, under such circumstances the active life of the Christian man in this world can become a 'means of grace' through which Jesus Christ Himself continually refreshes him with spiritual strength. We must not imagine that the devotional life is the place where we 'take in' something that at other times we 'give out'. The Christian life is not a matter of storing up inward accumulated resources through worship at one time and then dispensing them through active service. It is a matter of obeying the Word of God as it calls us both upward and outward, knowing that those who obey His Word and trust in His goodness will be sustained and used from moment to moment by the continual miracle of His free grace. Elijah is to be *sustained* by the command of God through

[1] Mark 9.2-29

the widow woman at Zarephath just as he was fed by the command of God through the ravens at Cherith. God will continue at Zarephath the same gracious ministry as he experienced at Cherith. God is seeking to minister to Elijah in body and soul through this widow woman as He ministered to him by the brook. Elijah needs her at this hour just as she needs him.

ELIJAH AND THE WIDOW

So he arose and went to Zarephath. And when he came to the gate of the city, behold, the widow woman was there gathering of sticks: and he called to her, and said, Fetch me, I pray thee, a little water in a vessel, that I may drink. And as she was going to fetch it, he called to her, and said, Bring me, I pray thee, a morsel of bread in thine hand. And she said, As the Lord thy God liveth, I have not a cake, but an handful of meal in a barrel, and a little oil in a cruse: and, behold, I am gathering two sticks, that I may go in and dress it for me and my son, that we may eat it and die. And Elijah said unto her, Fear not; go and do as thou hast said: but make me thereof a little cake first, and bring it unto me, and after make for thee and for thy son. For thus saith the Lord God of Israel, The barrel of meal shall not waste, neither shall the cruse of oil fail, until the day that the Lord sendeth rain upon the earth. And she went and did according to the saying of Elijah: and she, and he, and her house, did eat many days. And the barrel of meal wasted not, neither did the cruse of oil fail, according to the word of the Lord, which he spake by Elijah. And it came to pass after these things, that the son of the woman, the mistress of the house, fell sick; and his sickness was so sore, that there was no breath left in him. And she said unto Elijah, What have I to do with thee, O thou man of God? art thou come unto me to call my sin to remembrance, and to slay my son? And he said unto her, Give me thy son. And he took him out of her bosom, and carried him up into a loft, where he abode, and laid him upon his own bed. And he cried unto the Lord, and said, O Lord my God, hast thou also brought evil upon the widow with whom I sojourn, by slaying her son? And he stretched himself upon the child three times, and cried unto the Lord and said, O Lord my God, I pray thee, let this child's soul come into him again. And the Lord heard the voice of Elijah; and the soul of the child came into him again, and he revived. And Elijah took the child, and brought him down out of the chamber into the house, and delivered him unto his mother; and Elijah said, See, thy son liveth. And the woman said to Elijah, Now by this I know that thou art a man of God, and that the word of the Lord in thy mouth is truth.

I KINGS 17.10-24

When Elijah arrived at the home of the poor widow woman at Zarephath he must have been taken aback when God said,

'Here is the widow whom I have commanded to sustain thee!' She was at the point of death. She was gathering sticks for what she feared would be the last meal she and her son could ever hope for on this earth. She had had no vision that told her God would be sending His prophet to her door. Yet the Word of the Lord said to Elijah, 'Here is the house I have provided for thy shelter. Here is the woman I have commanded to sustain thee!' How hard it was for him to believe that this, the first desperate poor woman he met in this desolate spot, was indeed the angel who was to minister to him in body and soul during the critical weeks and months that lay ahead!

How hard it is for us to grasp the fact today that Jesus Christ is seeking to get into our lives to help us by surrounding us by poor, despised, broken and desperate specimens of humanity. His teaching tells us that we are always in desperate need of His help and that we will often find Him seeking to help us through those around us who seem least likely to give us help! That is why He told the vivid story of Dives the rich man who neglected Lazarus[1] the beggar at his gate only to find out in the afterlife that God had put Lazarus there to be his friend in his need as a rich man. And that is also one of the reasons why He told the parable of the sheep and the goats,[2] where we are reminded that He Himself may be there accosting us in His power to save us when we are faced with the sick, the naked, the poor, the imprisoned in all their need. We must learn that God is seeking to minister His grace to us, sometimes through the most unlikely channels. If instead of shunning those around us who at first sight are needy and desperate, we would open our hearts to their need and their influence, we might find that they are the ministers of God to us, and that they bring with themselves, into our lives, abundant spiritual wealth.

The widow woman no less than Elijah must have been taken aback when she realised that God had chosen her in all her weakness and desperation to serve Him at this juncture in the destiny of His people, and that God was to transform her last feeble act of self-preservation into a glorious service of His name. When Jesus preached a sermon in the synagogue at

---

[1] Luke 16.19-31   [2] Matt. 25.31-46

Capernaum on this story of Elijah and the widow, this was the point in the story that He brought out. This woman was the most unlikely person in the whole land to be used by God to help Elijah.[1] She was not even an Israelite. She could be counted amongst the poorest and most insignificant of all God's people. And yet it was she who was chosen! How privileged she was when God brought Elijah to her door! Insignificant, nameless she was, yet God had a great and divine work for her to do!

We ourselves must not despair if at times we feel very like her in our weakness. We tend to grow despondent because we feel that God needs good and capable people for His service, and we wonder how we could ever qualify to be of use for Him. We doubt if we have any resources at all to put at His disposal. But the miracle is that God can use the weak to minister to the strong. God wanted to use Lazarus, loathsome in sores, to minister to opulent Dives. He used a very ordinary man like Ananias to give the Apostle Paul the friendship and encouragement that he needed at the crisis of his life when he was still blind from his encounter on the Damascus Road and was desperately in need of someone to befriend and guide him.[2] No wonder that when the same Apostle Paul thought of his own weakness and surveyed the extraordinary things God had done through his own ministry, he summed up his thoughts about it by saying: 'God hath chosen the foolish things of the world to confound the wise; and God hath chosen the weak things of the world to confound the things which are mighty; And base things of the world, and things which are despised, hath God chosen.'[3]

MERCY OR JUDGMENT?

Elijah's stay at the house at Zarephath was blessed from the start by a sign of God's favour and mercy. In faith and trembling the widow devoted the last handful of meal and the last drop of oil to serving first the prophet and then herself and her son, and the Word of the Lord through Elijah was fulfilled: '*The barrel of meal wasted not, neither did the cruse of oil fail.*' Nothing could have been more miraculous or have given more certain evidence that Elijah was in truth a man held by God

[1] Luke 4.25-6   [2] Acts 9.10-19   [3] 1 Cor. 1.27-8

for His service and brought by God to her door than this token of the never-failing oil and meal.

But soon a crisis took place. There occurred an apparent sign of God's anger and judgment that nearly shattered the faith of the widow and must have sorely assailed the faith of Elijah himself. '*And it came to pass, after these things, that the son of the woman, the mistress of the house, fell sick; and his sickness was so sore, that there was no breath left in him.*' What was the poor woman to think as she watched her child die in this home that had seemed to be so singularly blessed by the presence and favour of God? How was she to interpret these two signs, the everlasting barrel of meal and the sudden and tragic death of her son? When Elijah had arrived at her home the urgent question in her mind had been, 'Who is this God, who has brought His prophet to the door of my house? What is His nature?' she had wondered. 'Is He a loving God or an angry one?' God had shown Himself towards the people of Israel as an angry God, who sent terrible punishment for the sins of men. Her instinct at first had been to have nothing to do with this man of God when he came to her door, for the Lord was a God who had brought famine to Israel, a God who was righteous and punished iniquity. She remembered that until this man of God had come with his stern preaching there had been prosperity in Israel.

Such were her thoughts when Elijah appeared at her door, and yet she had finally received him in faith that the Lord had sent him in mercy. But now here was a fresh sign of His judgment and anger against her. Could she now continue to trust in His love in face of this fresh sign of His anger? Was His word mockery or was it truth? Was He indeed a God who delighted in mercy or a God who delighted in judgment?

She found it hard, this inner conflict in her faith. In her first spasm of grief, giving way to doubt, she felt that it was the man of God who was responsible for bringing this judgment to her home. God has sent him to condemn her sin, rather than to save her life. She said to Elijah, '*What have I to do with thee, O thou man of God? art thou come unto me to call my sin to remembrance, and to slay my son?*' Was it not better that she should have nothing to do with him at all, than to suffer this tragedy by being near to the man of God?

It was a crisis, not only for the woman, but also for Elijah's faith. What was he to answer? Had the Lord indeed brought evil upon this woman's house? Elijah was in agony of mind and heart. How was he to face or answer this woman? He agonised over this problem as he prayed over the body of the dead child.

In our Christian life we are constantly being subjected to the same test as were Elijah and this woman. We are certainly surrounded by innumerable signs of God's mercy towards us. We can experience today miracles of God's power to answer our prayers to heal us and to provide for our needs. Such miracles as we experience today are only a small degree less spectacular than that performed in the house at Zarephath. How many Christians are there today who could testify that time and again in life when they were destitute God had provided for their needs through answers to prayer that were quite supernatural and wonderful. How many concrete proofs are there of the reality of 'divine healing' in cases which had been given up by the medical profession. How many signs are there in the social life of our land of the power of Jesus Christ to change human nature and to elevate human living.

Yet we are also surrounded by other signs that raise dark questions in our minds about the meaning of life and the meaning of everything that God has hitherto done for us and which we have interpreted as coming from His mercy. We are faced with the problem of why the innocent seem to suffer more than the wicked. We are faced with the problem of the continuing prevalence of death with its tragic and bitter consequences in a world where it is proclaimed to us in the Gospel that Christ has banished death! We are faced too with the dark manifestations of the power of evil to distort God's creation in ways that seem quite devilish. We are faced with the possibility of atomic warfare and a ghastly end to civilisation.

So we live with our faith continually being tested. Are we to believe that the signs we see of God's love and faithfulness are His true and final Word to us—or is He too at work mocking us in the other signs of corruption and death and chaos that seem to give a lie to the signs of His love?

At times we can become so oppressed by the conflicting

evidence around us that we find faith as difficult as did this widow. Certainly when God answers our prayers and works with power in our circumstances, opening doors before us and removing obstacles that were in our way, we can rise to great heights of joyful assurance and faith. And yet how soon can something else happen that we cannot fit into any scheme of things that we can believe to be ordered by love. How soon can we fall from the heights of faith to become almost overwhelmed in the depths of despair, to cry out like the father of the epileptic boy, 'Lord, I believe; help thou mine unbelief.'[1]

THE SIGN OF RESURRECTION

All the dark problems that passed through the mind of the widow and Elijah as they weighed the sign of God's mercy against the sign of God's judgment and wondered at His providence were finally and gloriously solved in the third sign that God gave during Elijah's stay at Zarephath. It was given in answer to Elijah's agonising prayer as he stretched himself out upon the child and cried out to God to restore his life. '*And the Lord heard the voice of Elijah; and the soul of the child came into him again, and he revived.*'

'*And the woman said to Elijah, Now by this I know that thou art a man of God, and that the word of the Lord in thy mouth is truth.*' By this third sign of resurrection both Elijah and the widow knew that the Word of God is truth indeed. If it promises us blessing, it gives us blessing indeed. They did not need to be afraid in dealing with God, as if there were two different sides to Him. He is not at one time loving and just, and at another capricious and spiteful. He does not show Himself one day merciful towards His people only to let them find on the next that He has had another whim and is now angry with them. His promises are not yea and then nay, but always yea and amen.

The Resurrection of Jesus Christ from the dead must be for us God's final answer to all our own problems about God's providence. The Resurrection of Christ is God's last glorious and triumphant sign to all who will believe that He *is* a God of love and faithfulness, that He *has* conquered death and defeated all the powers of evil. The Resurrection of Christ

[1] Mark 9.24

shows us that all our answers to prayer, all our experiences of divine healing, all the other wonderful works of Jesus in this world, are due to the fact that in Him the power of God and the life of the new creation have broken once for all into this world in irresistible reality. The Resurrection of Christ proves to us that the presence of death and decay and corruption, the apparent continuance of the power of evil with all the dark signs it can produce, need no longer destroy our faith, for the power of evil has been defeated in the decisive battle, the sting of death has been taken away, and all things are moving towards the day when God's triumph shall be fully manifest. The Resurrection of Christ shows us that God who raised up Jesus from the dead is indeed faithful to all who commit themselves body and soul to Him, and that His last Word to those who trust Him is never death but life, never judgment but mercy.

SEARCHLIGHT ON THE HIDDEN CHURCH

And it came to pass after many days, that the word of the Lord came to Elijah in the third year, saying, Go, shew thyself unto Ahab; and I will send rain upon the earth. And Elijah went to shew himself unto Ahab. And there was a sore famine in Samaria. And Ahab called Obadiah, which was the governor of his house. (Now Obadiah feared the Lord greatly: For it was so, when Jezebel cut off the prophets of the Lord that Obadiah took an hundred prophets, and hid them by fifty in a cave, and fed them with bread and water.) And Ahab said unto Obadiah, Go into the land, unto all fountains of water, and unto all brooks: peradventure we may find grass to save the horses and mules alive, that we lose not all the beasts. So they divided the land between them, to pass throughout it: Ahab went one way by himself, and Obadiah went another way by himself. And as Obadiah was in the way, behold, Elijah met him: and he knew him, and fell on his face, and said, Art thou that my lord Elijah? And he answered him, I am: go, tell thy lord, Behold, Elijah is here. And he said, What have I sinned, that thou wouldest deliver thy servant into the hand of Ahab, to slay me? As the Lord thy God liveth, there is no nation or kingdom, whither my lord hath not sent to seek thee: and when they said, He is not there; he took an oath of the kingdom and nation, that they found thee not. And now thou sayest, Go, tell thy lord, Behold, Elijah is here. And it shall come to pass, as soon as I am gone from thee, that the Spirit of the Lord shall carry thee whither I know not; and so when I come and tell Ahab, and he cannot find thee, he shall slay me: but I thy servant fear the Lord from my youth. Was it not told my lord what I did when Jezebel slew the prophets of the Lord, how I hid an hundred men of the Lord's prophets by fifty in a cave, and fed them with bread and water? And now thou sayest, Go, tell thy lord, Behold, Elijah is here: and he shall slay me. And Elijah said, As the Lord of hosts liveth, before whom I stand, I will surely shew myself unto him today. So Obadiah went to meet Ahab, and told him: and Ahab went to meet Elijah.

I KINGS 18.1-16

THE TIME FOR ACTION

'*And it came to pass after many days, that the word of the Lord came to Elijah in the third year, saying, Go, shew thyself unto Ahab; and I will send rain upon the earth.*' For three years God had done nothing drastic to alter the religious and political situation in Israel. Elijah, the man prepared to meet and master the situation had been hidden by God and kept in silence and inactivity. He himself must have wondered why his God waited so long. But now the day and the hour that God has chosen have arrived and Elijah is sent forth. Since it is God's time, everything has to be done with devastating thoroughness, and there is a dramatic opening of the movement that is to bring the house of Ahab crashing to the ground.

We do not have the same periods of long and dreary waiting for God's time as had the men of the Old Testament. The New Testament makes it clear that since Jesus Christ died and rose again, *now* is always the appointed time for salvation, for going forth to sow the seed of the Word of God, for responding to that Word with faith and repentance, with love and service. God forbid that any of us should ever imagine that we have to wait *many days* before we respond to the imperative challenge of the living Jesus Christ to decision and action in His name!

Yet there may be circumstances under which even we have to refrain from taking what seems obvious action till we have become certain, through waiting upon God in humility and patience, that God's time for such action has come. Doing little things at the right time can be a much more important contribution to the Kingdom of God than creating a great stir at the wrong time or even all the time. For certain tasks and undertakings one time is certainly better than another. There are times when little can be achieved by much effort, times when spectacular results can come through little effort.

Let us remember too that for the final day of redemption, and for the full manifestation of His Kingdom and glory, God may seem to make us wait long and indefinitely. Vileness and corruption may seem to be widespread, things may seem to be settled for ever in favour of evil. But God is not indifferent. He is waiting for the situation to become ripe for His action. He is waiting to give men time to repent. He is waiting for the hour to strike when He will be able to act with shattering completeness of judgment upon the whole set-up of evil.

'When the fullness of the time was come,' said Paul, 'God sent forth his Son.'[1] It was long after His servants had grown

---
[1] Gal. 4.4

weary with waiting and watching that Christ came to this earth to redeem it, yet it was the fullness of time. God never makes mistakes in His time, and even if, as Jesus prophesied in the vivid parable of the ten virgins,[1] the bridegroom should come at the last possible hour when all semblance of expectancy and hope have faded out of the hearts of those who have no true faith, it will not be too late!

The Miracle of the Hidden Church

'*Elijah went to shew himself unto Ahab.*' He went forth apparently alone to challenge in the name of God, the powers of evil that were so triumphant, so strongly entrenched, deep in the life of Israel, so apparently unconquerable. Let us not underestimate the courage of this man as he went forth to show himself to Ahab. Ahab had sent his men to scour the land for Elijah. Ahab had sworn hundreds of times to bring about Elijah's death. In Ahab's mind, and to Ahab's way of thinking, Elijah was responsible for the terrible famine that had ruined his kingdom and spoilt his planned economy. If anywhere in the Old Testament we have a foreshadowing of what Jesus Christ did when he set His face steadfastly to go to Jerusalem to face His Cross and to lay down His challenge to the powers of evil, then surely it is here in this picture of Elijah going apparently alone to face Ahab, Jezebel, the priests of Baal, and the bewildered and resentful nation.

Yet as Elijah went forth we are shown that though he was indeed alone and seemed destined to fight this battle with evil single-handed, he was nevertheless not the only one in Israel who cared greatly for God, and who was deeply concerned to maintain the true faith and overcome Baal. At the end of the next chapter we are to be told that in spite of all appearances to the contrary there was a large hidden Church in Israel. There were many of the nation who had been secretly waiting, hoping and praying for the new day. 'Yet have I seven thousand in Israel all the knees that have not bowed to Baal and all the lips that have not kissed him,' was God's news to this depressed and lonely prophet.

We have already seen signs of the existence of this hidden Church in the simple piety of the widow woman at Zarephath,

[1] Matt. 25.1-13

and now, just before Elijah goes forth to his task of standing alone for the cause of God at the great hour of decision and crisis, as if to reveal this encouraging though distant background of support, a searchlight seems to fall on another part of this hidden Church. We are informed that there are a hundred true prophets of God somewhere in hiding and we are shown in bold relief Obadiah, the governor of Ahab's household: '*And Ahab called Obadiah, which was the governor of his house. (Now Obadiah feared the Lord greatly: For it was so, when Jezebel cut off the prophets of the Lord that Obadiah took an hundred prophets . . ., and fed them with bread and water.)*'

The existence of this hidden Church is a miracle. '*Obadiah feared the Lord greatly*,' yet he lived in Ahab's palace, at the very centre of Baal worship. Obadiah did not bow the knee to Baal. He lived in an atmosphere of jealousy, lust and spite—how could the court of Jezebel and Ahab have any other atmosphere?—and yet he kept his faith. Obadiah's consistent presence as a God-fearing man at the court of King Ahab is a miracle no less than the great miracle that Elijah was so soon to accomplish on Mount Carmel. In the midst of an environment that was pagan and hostile to all true godliness, God proved adequate to keeping the man who trusted in Him. Moreover, God gave Obadiah favour in the eyes of Ahab. Some commentators express surprise that Ahab should have employed a man who was so dedicated to the faith he himself was trying to destroy. But Ahab employed Obadiah simply because he could be depended upon and because God Himself gave him favour in the eyes of others. 'When a man's ways please the Lord, he maketh even his enemies to be at peace with him.'[1] God has varied ways of preserving a Church for Himself on earth.

There are many parallels in the Bible to Obadiah at the court of King Ahab. We can think of Daniel in the court of the kings of Babylonia and Persia. Daniel set his heart to fear the Lord and to understand God's laws, and God kept him a man of faith and prayer and true integrity, and made him a man of real influence with such widely differing monarchs as Nebuchadnezzar, Belshazzar and Darius. In Paul's Epistle to the Philippians he speaks of the saints 'that are of Caesar's

---

[1] Prov. 16.7

household'.[1] There in the midst of the imperial palace, the centre of life that was in so many ways antagonistic to the Christian faith, God nevertheless had His people, and His power kept them as saints.

If God kept His hidden Church in the days of Elijah faithful in the midst of the fiercest temptation to bow the knee to Baal, He can also keep His people today faithful in the midst of any modern environment. We hear it often stated that our modern industrial civilisation is becoming an increasingly impossible environment in which to expect men to live as Christians, and in which to preach a call to individuals to be Christians. It is true that many Christian men do their daily work under conditions and influences that produce a continual temptation to compromise in a way that betrays their faith. Many on Monday morning are forced to face a world that is entirely different in outlook and atmosphere from that within which they moved in the House of God on the Sabbath day. We must have real concern for the sake of the world in view of the widening gulf that is being created today between the Church and the world, yet we must not despair for the sake of the Church in such a world.

To those who ask, Can a man really be a Christian in business and in society today? our answer must be that with man it is impossible. But here it is not simply a question of what man can do. It is a question of what God can do. With man it is impossible, but with God all things are possible, and one of these possible things is for God to enable those who trust in Him to live victoriously in this present world. Moreover, He can so give them His Spirit, that by His own gracious influence they gain the respect of others and take the leadership where confidence is lost in all else. It is because God is able to keep men thus by faith living in the main current of human life and yet not being swept away and lost in that current, that Paul is able to appeal to the Christians in Rome: 'Be not conformed to this world: but be ye transformed by the renewing of your mind.'[2] When He surveyed the Church in Sardis, at the time when the Book of Revelation was written, the Lord saw much to grieve Him. The very Church of Sardis had sunk almost to the low and sordid level of the pagan society around it, and yet all was

[1] Phil. 4.22   [2] Rom. 12.2

not black, for the Lord was able to say to the minister of His Church there, 'Thou hast a few names even in Sardis which have not defiled their garments'.[1]

THE FAILURE OF THE HIDDEN CHURCH

Yet the strange fact is that even though there were seven thousand in Israel who had not bowed the knee to Baal, it was one man alone who took vigorous political action and who by his political faithfulness saved the situation in Israel. The seven thousand did their duty in shunning participation in Baal worship, but they remained for the most part silent and unprotesting when some sign of their presence and some sound of united protest would have made it much easier for Elijah to champion the cause of the Lord. Elijah in the day when he challenged Ahab and Jezebel and saved Israel from their tyranny had to stand alone, wondering perhaps how much hidden support he had and where it lay, and wishing that there were others beside him to encourage him. No doubt the seven thousand helped by praying for Elijah. Without them he might not have succeeded. But none of them raised his voice in public when such a voice might have made all the difference to the course of political events.

Elijah obviously did not want to stand entirely alone. He tried to enlist Obadiah on his side when he met him. '*Go, tell thy lord, Behold, Elijah is here.*' We can imagine that this was an appeal for support. Obadiah might be able to make things a little easier for him with Ahab. But Obadiah was afraid. If he went to tell Ahab that he had met Elijah, Ahab might think that he had been responsible for hiding Elijah during the past three years and might kill him in anger. In any case the news that Elijah had reappeared was bad news for Ahab and he might kill Obadiah as the bearer of it. Moreover, Elijah had a way of disappearing and reappearing under the protection of God that made things easier for him than for an ordinary man like Obadiah. Besides this Obadiah was not sure of Elijah. Elijah was a man extreme in his views and strange in his conduct who tended to alienate support rather than encourage it. All these thoughts may have gone through Obadiah's mind and made him hesitate at this critical moment.

[1] Rev. 3.4

He gave Elijah some help, but ultimately the searchlight that shone on Obadiah and picked him out in such bright and hopeful colours passed on, leaving him again in the darkness and focused on Elijah alone. We know there was a hidden Church in Israel, a Church with men of great devotion and piety whose existence was a miracle of God's grace, but nevertheless it was not great enough to come fully into the light and meet the political challenge of the times. What had to be done in that sphere was to be done by one man alone.

It makes us marvel all the more at the courage of Elijah, who could persist in a course of action whose danger made even a man like Obadiah tremble. But it also gives us cause for some reflection on the failure of this Church of the seven thousand to stand by Elijah in the great day of crisis—and on our own failure in our own day to take Christian action in the sphere of politics.

The Church of Christ can never perish but it can become hidden and thus less effective on the life of the world than it need be. If the church is to retain its influence in shaping human history, it must realise afresh how closely politics and the Kingdom of God are related. The Word of God must be allowed to interferé with the public life of our times as well as with the private lives of individual Christians. And this means that the Church must continually speak out boldly and courageously on political matters, and must be watchful over all the policies of governments. It is not enough for Christians to pray for the State and to carry in their hearts a burden of mourning because of the public sins of their day. They must also lift up their voice against all injustice and all immorality, in a protest that will be heard throughout the length and breadth of society. Obadiah's timid policy of refusing to interfere in politics was not enough. We cannot separate religion and politics. The Church in his day would have been throttled by a political manœuvre in spite of all his piety and in spite of all the fervent religion of the seven thousand hidden servants of God had God not sent a man into the midst of the political arena to lift up his voice before the king and court; and unless today Christ has His men who are prepared to stand before the courts and kings and governments, prepared to write to the newspapers and to speak on public platforms in the name of their faith, all the piety of the Church by itself will not avail to stem the tide of advancing atheism.

The One who Stands Alone

Elijah's courage has reminded us of the courage of Jesus Christ in facing His Cross. His solitude reminds us of the solitude and isolation of Him who in the Garden of Gethsemane found that even His closest disciples could not watch with Him for one hour, and who on The Cross in His final conflict with evil found no one beside Him and suffered alone. In every age of Israel's history God looked for those who could represent Him and fulfil the task of His servant to their generation. Sometimes He found one outstanding prophet, sometimes He found a small group of the faithful, a mere remnant of the whole nation. When the time came for the fulfilment of the purpose for which He had made Israel His people, He looked and could find no one to fulfil His purpose or to do His task for Him, and so He came Himself to be the true Israel in His own Person, to bear what no other could bear, to stand in and overcome in the conflict when all other men must fail. 'And he saw that there was no man, and wondered that there was no intercessor: therefore his arm brought salvation unto him; and his righteousness, it sustained him.'[1] 'When the fullness of the time was come, God sent forth his Son, made of a woman, made under the law. To redeem them that were under the law, that we might receive the adoption of sons.'[2]

[1] Isa. 59.16   [2] Gal. 4.4-5

DECISION AT MOUNT CARMEL

And it came to pass, when Ahab saw Elijah, that Ahab said unto him, Art thou he that troubleth Israel? And he answered, I have not troubled Israel; but thou, and thy father's house, in that ye have forsaken the commandments of the Lord, and thou hast followed Baalim. Now therefore send, and gather to me all Israel unto mount Carmel, and the prophets of Baal four hundred and fifty, and the prophets of the groves four hundred, which eat at Jezebel's table. So Ahab sent unto all the children of Israel, and gathered the prophets together unto mount Carmel. And Elijah came unto all the people, and said, How long halt ye between two opinions? if the Lord be God, follow him: but if Baal, then follow him. And the people answered him not a word. Then said Elijah unto the people, I, even I only, remain a prophet of the Lord; but Baal's prophets are four hundred and fifty men. Let them therefore give us two bullocks; and let them choose one bullock for themselves, and cut it in pieces, and lay it on wood, and put no fire under: and I will dress the other bullock, and lay it on wood, and put no fire under: And call ye on the name of your gods, and I will call on the name of the Lord: and the God that answereth by fire, let him be God. And all the people answered and said, It is well spoken. And Elijah said unto the prophets of Baal, Choose you one bullock for yourselves, and dress it first; for ye are many; and call on the name of your gods, but put no fire under. And they took the bullock which was given them, and they dressed it, and called on the name of Baal from morning even until noon, saying, O Baal, hear us. But there was no voice, nor any that answered. And they leaped upon the altar which was made. And it came to pass at noon, that Elijah mocked them, and said, Cry aloud: for he is a god; either he is talking, or he is pursuing, or he is in a journey, or peradventure he sleepeth, and must be awaked. And they cried aloud, and cut themselves after their manner with knives and lancets, till the blood gushed out upon them. And it came to pass, when midday was past, and they prophesied until the time of the offering of the evening sacrifice, that there was neither voice, nor any to answer, nor any that regarded. And Elijah said unto all the people, Come near unto me. And all the people came near unto him. And he repaired the altar of the Lord that was broken down. And Elijah took twelve stones, according to the number of the tribes of the sons of Jacob, unto whom the word of the Lord came, saying, Israel shall be thy name: And with the stones he built an altar in the name of the Lord: and he made a trench about the altar, as great as would contain two measures of seed. And he put the wood in order, and cut the bullock in pieces, and laid him on the wood, and said, Fill four barrels with water, and pour it on the burnt sacrifice, and on the wood. And he said, Do it the second time. And they did it the second time. And he said, Do it the third time. And they did it the third time. And the water ran round about the altar; and he filled the trench also with water. And it came to pass at the time of the offering of the evening sacrifice, that Elijah the prophet came near, and said, Lord God of Abraham, Isaac, and of Israel, let it be known this day that thou art God in Israel, and that I am thy servant, and that I have done all these things at thy word. Hear me, O Lord, hear me, that this people may know that thou art the Lord God, and that thou hast turned their heart back again. Then the fire of the Lord fell, and consumed the burnt sacrifice, and the wood, and the stones, and the dust, and licked up the water that was in the trench. And when all the people saw it, they fell on their faces: and they said, The Lord, he is the God; the Lord, he is the God. And Elijah said unto them, Take the prophets of Baal; let not one of them escape. And they took them: and Elijah brought them down to the brook Kishon, and slew them there. And Elijah said unto Ahab, Get thee up, eat and drink; for there is a sound of abundance of rain. So Ahab went up to eat and to drink. And Elijah went up to the top of Carmel; and he cast himself down upon the earth, and put his face between his knees, and said to his servant, Go up now, look toward the sea. And he went up, and looked, and said, There is nothing. And he said, Go again seven times. And it came to pass at the seventh time, that he said, Behold, there ariseth a little cloud out of the sea, like a man's hand. And he said, Go up, say unto Ahab, Prepare thy chariot, and get thee down, that the rain stop thee not. And it came to pass in the mean while, that the heaven was black with clouds and wind, and there was a great rain.

1 KINGS 18.17-45

BOTH . . . AND?

History has proved that man undoubtedly has an 'instinct for religion'. If he does not have a god he will make one. If he has a god and finds that god unsatisfying he will make another one or two to give himself satisfaction. Or he will adopt someone else's god besides his own. For man has often found the worship of only one god rather a dull affair. Therefore he has sought to introduce variety into his religious life. 'There be gods many, and lords many,'[1] wrote Paul to the Corinthians, commenting on the extraordinary number and

[1] 1 Cor. 8.5

complexity of the gods and religions that he found around him in the Greek world of his time.

The people of Israel at this time in their history had given way to this lust for religious variety and excitement. The Lord was 'one God only'. That was not interesting enough. The services He commanded were dull and extremely puritanical compared with the sensuous and sensual rites that attracted huge crowds around the pagan temples in the world of the time. Why not add some variety to the religious life of Israel? After all, they were famous for their religion. Let them have a good one to boast about. They had had a royal marriage recently. Ahab had married Jezebel and had brought her home amidst great national rejoicing. Jezebel's god was Baal. Here was an exciting new religion ready-made with scores of Tyrian priests willing to come and teach all the orgies and ceremonies free of charge! Why not adopt Baal as well as the Lord, and so have a breadth and variety of religious life in Israel that would put all other nations in the shade? The people of Israel welcomed Baal as they had welcomed Jezebel. They built altars to him, bowed the knee to him, and kissed him. Why not? They did not give up the Lord for all this. They kept the Lord as their chief national God. He came first. His temple was of course always full, always well kept up. But it was the Lord *and* Baal. Their priests told them that they could worship both gods. Indeed, some said that the ideas they culled from Baal worship would in the long run enrich their own ideas of the Lord, and help to embellish and improve their national tradition in religion. Why not?

The same kind of question and temptation came to the early Christians in the Roman world. They had Jesus Christ. They had their Bible which witnessed to Him as Lord and from the study of which they had to build up their faith and their Christian life and form their traditions of worship. But all around them in the Greek and Roman world there were multitudes of gods and religions and philosophies. Some, it is true, were bad, but some seemed good. Some were stupid and immoral, but others were highly intellectual and moral. Could a Christian with discernment not worship Jesus Christ *and* at the same time pay some homage to what was best in the pagan religion of the Roman Empire? Why not? And why not enrich the religion taught in the Bible with ideas culled from the noblest Greek philosophy and the highest Roman moral culture? Why not improve the religious ceremonies taught in the New Testament by adding some attractive bits from the rituals observed in the pagan temples around them. And when times of persecution came and they were threatened with death unless they threw a handful of incense on a pagan altar and bowed the knee to the Emperor—why not? Why should that necessarily mean giving up the Lord? Why not have the Lord *and* something else in addition?

Today we are still faced with the same pressing question. We still have Jesus Christ of course. He is Lord, we say. But there are many other altars at which men can bow the knee besides that of Christ and many other temples in which men can worship besides that of the true Lord. In the Sermon on the Mount Jesus warned us about a God called Mammon. The worship of Mammon is being carried on in the modern world on a very large scale in circles where money and personal advancement are being ruthlessly pursued as ends in themselves. But why not?

The worship of the goddess Venus is another cult as highly popular in our day as in the old days of Greece and Rome. Whenever and wherever in the press or on the stage, for example, the sex element in life is exalted out of all proportion to its true place in God's scheme of things, an altar is being set up to Venus and men are being called on to invoke and worship her. But why not bow the knee to Venus? men ask—as long as we do not at the same time forsake Jesus Christ!

Any list of the religions of the modern world would be inadequate unless it referred to the cult of gambling. The gambler 'magnifies the place of chance in his life', says a recent Church pamphlet on the subject. Undoubtedly the big gambler magnifies it till it has the proportions of a god. 'Gambling is the only big thing of my week; other things now have little interest for me. I play to win and in winning is my satisfaction' is a typical statement from a confirmed gambler, quoted in the same pamphlet. But most devotees of the gambling cult are not yet confirmed. They spend only a small sum each week. There is nothing more in it than throwing a mere handful of incense on the altar of possible 'good luck'.

DECISION AT MOUNT CARMEL

Why not? Why should a Christian worry about a little indulgence in the cult of chance—as long as he does not at the same time forsake Jesus Christ?

Jesus Christ *and* Mammon; Jesus Christ *and* Venus; Jesus Christ *and* Chance. The Lord *and* Baal—why not?

EITHER . . . OR!

Elijah's plan of action in this situation was deliberately spectacular. He provoked a tensely dramatic crisis in the life of his nation. He created a situation in which the issues were so clarified for the onlooking people that they found themselves forced to make a final choice between the Lord and Baal. '*Now therefore send*,' he cried to Ahab, '*and gather to me all Israel unto mount Carmel, and the prophets of Baal . . . which eat at Jezebel's table.*' He precipitated a spectacular life or death struggle between himself and the priests of Baal in which one and only one side could possibly win. He produced the situation in which God if He willed could visibly vindicate His name and decisively and supernaturally speak for Himself.

It is a great scene. The whole nation is gathered. We have Elijah standing alone for God and the prophets of Baal standing on the other side in their hundreds, and we have the undecided mass of people who have so far tried to please both sides, looking on with awe and fear of what is to happen.

Elijah began by preaching. His sermon was short, clear and right to the point. No one ever forgot his final words of appeal and warning that hushed the whole assembly into a troubled silence. '*How long hop ye between two opinions?*' he cried in mockery, '*If the Lord be God, follow him: but if Baal, then follow him.*'

He tried with all the passion and eloquence he had to make the men of his time see that it must be *either* the Lord *or* Baal, but *never* both. He tried to convince them that to cultivate a religious life that involved a continual traffic between the House of the Lord and the house of some other god was to make a mockery both of faith in God and of life itself. Such a religion has no reality. It springs from a view of life that refuses to take anything seriously, for instead of looking on life as a sphere where decision has real meaning and where real *decision* has to be made, it leads to a view of life as a mere game in which men are always hopping about uncomfortably on one leg from one thing to another with no hope of finding any final rest or true solidity anywhere.

How stupid of the Israelites to think that they could go on for ever halting between two opinions in this way without making unintelligent fools of themselves! How stupid of them to think that they could continue the compromise without further terrible judgment from Him whose Word is, 'Thou shalt have no other gods before me!'[1]

The task of the preacher of the Gospel, and the task of the Church today, is still to trouble and disturb men as Elijah did by pressing for decision between Jesus Christ and every other lord men are being tempted to set up and devote themselves to alongside Him. It is to say clearly to men who want *both* Jesus Christ *and* another, '*How long halt ye between two opinions?*' *Either* Jesus Christ *or* another, but *never both*! We must show men today, as Elijah did in his times, how stupid it is to confess at one moment that Jesus is Lord and God and all, and then turn from him and His Word to seek elsewhere some new bit of wisdom or religious excitement in order to try to add this to what we already have in Him. What a ludicrous piece of unreal ritual our Church service becomes on Sunday, when during the week without any shame of conscience we can throw even a handful of incense on the altar of some other supposed god, be it in the cult of Mammon or Venus or Chance or any other!

It is easier for us today than it was for Elijah in his time to confront men with this great *either-or*. When we appeal today for decision in the name of Christ, we do not need to plan to bring men into any kind of dramatic situation in which they will be able vividly to see the issues on which they are to decide, for we have the Cross of Jesus Christ to point to and to preach about. Through the preaching of the Cross in every generation God faces men with the issues on which they must decide who is to be lord of their lives. Through the preaching of the Cross in every generation the living Christ forces Himself upon the judgment of men and thus judges them by their judgment of Himself. In the Cross God has shown clearly for every generation of mankind how impossible it is to try to be

[1] Exod. 20.3

neutral towards the totalitarian claims of Jesus Christ—how impossible it is to compromise with the pride or the religion or the lust or the greed or the carelessness which crucified Him. How can we turn from the Cross to indulge in anything that is a rival to Jesus Christ? Our task in bringing men to decision is to bring them to the Cross and there to say, 'Jesus Christ alone can be your Lord'.

THE FIRE FROM HEAVEN

It was not the sermon that brought the men of Israel to decision. It was the fire from Heaven. '*The God that answereth by fire, let him be God.*' Elijah's preaching failed in spite of his passionate eloquence and sincerity. '*The people answered him not a word.*' Elijah at that hour was made to realise the limitations even of the most eloquent and dramatic preaching. When three years' famine had failed to change the hearts of Israel, one short sermon by itself could avail little. If Israel was to be converted God must speak for Himself and give His witness from Heaven.

Elijah was sure that God would speak for Himself. He must have felt, in some way we cannot understand, guided and constrained by God to challenge Him to send the fire, for he staked everything that day not on his own efforts or his own eloquence, but on his faith that God Himself would speak in His own way. In vivid contrast to the priests of Baal who jumped about ecstatically and cut themselves with knives and shouted wild and anxious prayers to Baal in the direction of heaven, Elijah was calm and collected. '*Hear me, O Lord, hear me,*' he cried quietly and confidently in his final prayer of invocation, '*that this people may know that Thou art the Lord God, and that thou hast turned their heart back again*'.

It was this calm faith that God honoured. '*The fire of the Lord fell, and consumed the burnt sacrifice, and the wood, and the stones, and the dust, and licked up the water that was in the trench. And when all the people saw it, they fell on their faces; and they said, The Lord, he is the God; the Lord, he is the God.*'

If we are to convince men of the reality of God today, mere preaching—even the preaching of the Cross of Christ—is not enough by itself. How often today has the minister in his sermon been eloquent and true to the witness of the Bible, but '*the people answered him not a word*'. If the people are to answer, then the fire of the Holy Ghost must fall from Heaven into our midst as we point men to behold the one true sacrifice —'the Lamb of God, which taketh away the sin of the world'.[1]

And we have been promised this fire from Heaven as we face the world today in the name of Christ and point to His Cross and call on men to decide whether that indeed is the true sacrifice. 'I indeed baptize you with water,' said John the Baptist to his disciples, 'but . . . He shall baptize you with the Holy Ghost, and with fire.'[2] This promise was fulfilled when the fire of the Spirit fell on the Church at Pentecost.[3] And though we need expect no sound as of a rushing mighty wind, no manifest visible tongues of flame, nevertheless the coming of the Holy Ghost whom the fire and the wind symbolised is His promise for ever to His Church, and to those who stand before men lifting up His Cross. 'I, if I be lifted up from the earth, will draw all men unto me.'[4]

Since we have all these promises that God will send His fire, how confident we can be in facing our task of witnessing to God in this world. Surely God will honour His Word and make us not ashamed as we set about trying to convince men of His reality. The contrast between the calm behaviour of Elijah, and the strained excited and exaggerated behaviour of the priests of Baal should be a warning to us and a lesson. But here is where we fail. Instead of acting and speaking in calm faith, trusting not in our own powers but in God's promise to be with us, we, like the priests of Baal, tend in our desperation to try artificial and dramatic means of impressing the onlookers. We try by clever technique to produce our own fire from Heaven and our own emotional effect. In our nervousness we may try by desperate activity or forced effort of prayer even to compel God to send His fire. But the true fire of God that will convert men does not come in that way. It comes when men who have staked everything on God look up to Him, often quietly, and in 'confident despair' and true faith that they will not be ashamed because they wait upon Him. When men become too anxious to produce religious effect, we may be sure that it is because they lack real faith in the living God.

[1] John 1.29   [2] Matt. 3.11   [3] Acts 2   [4] John 12.32

When the fire fell it seemed to touch the hearts of the men of Israel as well as to consume the offering on the altar. Indeed, the fire itself was a symbol of the cleansing effect it was meant to produce that day in the hearts and lives of the people. '*The Lord, he is the God,*' they cried. No wonder they immediately responded to Elijah's call for ruthless action upon the priests of Baal. We prefer not to think too much of what their decision meant. But a true decision for God means not just making a confession of faith with our lips that the Lord is God, but also a ruthless clearing out of our lives of all that is incompatible with the Lordship of Jesus Christ over us. If Jesus Christ is Lord, then every idol must be cast down, and everything that is antagonistic to His Lordship must be attacked. When Jesus asserted His Lordship in the temple at Jerusalem he overturned the tables of the money changers and drove out those that bought and sold.[1] When Paul pointed out the scandals in the Church at Corinth and reasserted in their midst that Christ was Lord, it was with 'indignation . . . fear . . . vehement desire . . . zeal . . . revenge . . .' that they cleared themselves and their Church of the evil in their midst.[2] The Christian who exalts Christ as Lord in his own life is one who is bound to 'crucify'[3] the old nature and every inward tendency to go back to the rule of self. If Christ is Lord and the attitude of Jesus Christ to evil is true, then we must be as uncompromising and ruthless with evil in our life on the day of decision as Elijah was with the priests of Baal.

The coming of the fire was a sign to Elijah that the rain will soon follow. '*Get thee up, eat and drink,*' he cried to Ahab, '*for there is a sound of abundance of rain.*' The famine-stricken people needed this rain to save their homes and their lives as desperately as they had needed the fire to save their souls. Fire from Heaven can convince of the reality of the living God, but it cannot feed a hungry nation and restore their devastated fields. Israel is to learn again this day that the God, who sends fire to convert their hearts will also send rain to refresh and feed their bodies. For it is an unsatisfying and incomplete religion that thinks of God merely as the One who kindles religious emotions and gives great spiritual experiences in ecstatic moments in the house of prayer and worship, without

[1] Matt. 21.12 [2] 2 Cor. 7.11 [3] Gal. 5.24

following this during the week with the supply of man's concrete needs.

THE MAN OF PRAYER

Ahab and the rest of the people can now go and feast off the slender remains of their stores of food knowing that the rain is sure to come. But Elijah must still pray. '*Ahab went up to eat and to drink: and Elijah went up to the top of Carmel; and he cast himself upon the earth, and put his face between his knees.*' The fire had come in answer to Elijah's prayer. The rain will come only if Elijah continues to pray. How strange it is that in order to complete the work that God has begun and is bound to finish, Elijah must nevertheless still pray. Ahab and the rest of Israel can relax and rejoice, but Elijah must still watch in prayer and must still bear some measure of anxiety and agony. It is a lesson that many of us should ponder more carefully. We often relax too soon in the midst of Christian work. We forget that though God is determined and waiting to bless men, He must be besought with real fervency for the blessing He is waiting to bestow.

And here we see for a moment revealed the one secret that can give us in our day a share in doing things as great and wonderful as this mighty and distant man of God, Elijah. He worked wonders in his day not simply because he was a man caught up into a very special relationship with God, but also because he was a man who had learned to pray as we ourselves can learn to pray, and who out of love could throw himself on his face and make intercession for men who were either too weary or too unbelieving or too preoccupied to pray for their own dire needs. To imitate Elijah in any other respect is beyond us, but, the Apostle James reminds us, this privilege of being able to win God's blessing for men through prayer is beyond none of us who will have it. 'The effectual fervent prayer of a righteous man availeth much. Elias was a man subject to like passions as we are, and he prayed earnestly that it might not rain: and it rained not on the earth by the space of three years and six months. And he prayed again, and the heaven gave rain, and the earth brought forth her fruit.'[1]

[1] James 5.16-18

ELIJAH'S FLIGHT

And Ahab told Jezebel all that Elijah had done, and withal how he had slain all the prophets with the sword. Then Jezebel sent a messenger unto Elijah, saying, So let the gods do to me, and more also, if I make not thy life as the life of one of them by tomorrow about this time. And when he saw that, he arose, and went for his life, and came to Beer-sheba, which belongeth to Judah, and left his servant there. But he himself went a day's journey into the wilderness, and came and sat down under a juniper tree: and he requested for himself that he might die; and said, It is enough; now, O Lord, take away my life; for I am not better than my fathers. And as he lay and slept under a juniper tree, behold, then an angel touched him, and said unto him, Arise and eat. And he looked, and, behold, there was a cake baken on the coals, and a cruse of water at his head. And he did eat and drink, and laid him down again. And the angel of the Lord came again the second time, and touched him, and said, Arise and eat; because the journey is too great for thee. And he arose, and did eat and drink, and went in the strength of that meat forty days and forty nights unto Horeb the mount of God. And he came thither unto a cave, and lodged there; and, behold, the word of the Lord came to him, and he said unto him, What doest thou here, Elijah? And he said, I have been very jealous for the Lord God of hosts: for the children of Israel have forsaken thy covenant, thrown down thine altars, and slain thy prophets with the sword; and I, even I only, am left; and they seek my life, to take it away. And he said, Go forth, and stand upon the mount before the Lord. And, behold, the Lord passed by, and a great and strong wind rent the mountains, and brake in pieces the rocks before the Lord; but the Lord was not in the wind: and after the wind an earthquake; but the Lord was not in the earthquake: And after the earthquake a fire; but the Lord was not in the fire: and after the fire a still small voice. And it was so, when Elijah heard it, that he wrapped his face in his mantle, and went out, and stood in the entering in of the cave. And, behold, there came a voice unto him, and said, What doest thou here, Elijah? And he said, I have been very jealous for the Lord God of hosts: because the children of Israel have forsaken thy covenant, thrown down thine altars, and slain thy prophets with the sword; and I, even I only, am left; and they seek my life, to take it away. And the Lord said unto him, Go, return on thy way to the wilderness of Damascus: and when thou comest, anoint Hazael to be king over Syria: and Jehu the son of Nimshi shalt thou anoint to be king over Israel: and Elisha the son of Shaphat of

Abel-meholah shalt thou anoint to be prophet in thy room. And it shall come to pass, that him that escapeth the sword of Hazael shall Jehu slay: and him that escapeth from the sword of Jehu shall Elisha slay. Yet I have left me seven thousand in Israel, all the knees which have not bowed unto Baal, and every mouth which hath not kissed him.

I KINGS 19.1-18

FAILURE IN THE MIDST OF VICTORY

The Elijah we meet at the beginning of this chapter is a man who has just won a great victory for God. Only yesterday he challenged single-handed the forces of evil and struck a blow for God which was bound ultimately to bring the whole set-up of evil in Israel crashing to the ground. At the end of his day's work Ahab was terrified, the people were stirred up to a complete change of face, and four hundred and fifty priests of Baal were slain. At the end of the day Elijah must have thought himself the undisputed master of the situation. He must have seen visions of his nation reformed in its ways, purified in its worship, thronging the temple of the Lord with sincerity, and living according to its faith.

But all that took place in the last chapter. In the opening verses of this present one it had begun to appear that Elijah's success was not so complete after all. He had knocked the heart out of Ahab, and he had killed the prophets of Baal with the edge of the sword. But Ahab and the priests of Baal had been mere pawns in the hands of someone stronger than themselves. There was still the mastermind Jezebel to be dealt with, and when Jezebel walked in the whole scene seemed to change. She came prancing on to the stage, with her lips and face freshly painted, and her heart blazing with anger. Her will was set with iron determination. She had undergone a most humiliating defeat, but she had no intention of giving up the struggle. With her tenacity and resilience and determination in what was to her an hour of tragedy she can be an example to those of us who are tempted to grow despondent after frequent setbacks. What a woman she must have been, and what power she manifested at that time of crisis! She rallied her defeated forces, she whipped round her wavering lieutenants, and soon she was in a strong enough position to deliver her ultimatum to that upstart Elijah.

Elijah thus learned that no man can fight God's battles without being involved in humiliating defeat, even in what seems victory. The battle with the powers of evil is not one in which we can gain a victory and then have a rest, imagining that it will take the enemy time to recover. For the enemy we are engaging has enormous resources. If he suffers a setback on the field of this earth, he can soon arise and confront his challengers the next day, apparently fresh and inexhaustible, with a new and terrible challenge, and with such power that he seems able to make us fail in the hour of our victory.

Elijah cracked up. As we read on we see the man at whose courage all Israel had marvelled fleeing before the threat of a mere woman! We see the man who had spoken as if he had but to raise his hand and God would send legions of angels to aid him in the battle now floundering about for some prop by which to hold himself up. We see the man who had been the most spectacular political success suddenly sink into a mood of despondency and gloom.

Elijah was not the first man in Israel to break down in this way when he came hard up against the mystery of the power of evil to persist in the hearts of men. When Moses at the height of his career faced the same mystery he smashed the two tablets of stone in pieces on the mountain and vowed that he would be done with the whole business of serving God. King David in his battle for the Lord found himself so hated by his enemies that he wrote: 'Oh that I had wings like a dove! for then would I fly away, and be at rest. Lo, then would I wander far off, and remain in the wilderness. I would hasten my escape from the windy storm and tempest.'[1]

Elijah was so shattered in spirit that he wanted to die. *'He himself went a day's journey into the wilderness, and came and sat down under a juniper tree: and he requested for himself that he might die; and said, It is enough; now, O Lord, take away my life; for I am not better than my fathers.'* It had been life to Elijah to work for God. To give up working for God meant death. He felt he could no longer go on working for God on the battlefield of earth where the odds against him were so great. Elijah was no better than his fathers, Moses or David, when it came to standing up against the assaults of evil. Nor were his successors

[1] Ps. 55.6-8

among the prophets all men of iron in this respect. The great Jeremiah frequently echoes the cries of Moses, David and Elijah. And even serene Isaiah can write, 'I have laboured in vain, I have spent my strength for nought, and in vain'.[1]

VICTORY IN THE MIDST OF FAILURE

But God taught Elijah that He was and remained the victorious Lord in the midst of all this apparent failure. In spite of this set-back, in spite of Elijah's own despondency, in spite of all outward appearance to the contrary, God remained the calm and unembarrassed master of the situation in Israel.

From the start He took Elijah firmly in hand. He forced him to lie off his work and sent him away on a long holiday with an outward journey of forty days. Elijah was thus for many weeks put out of touch with the political and religious problems which he had thought he alone could solve; and he was not to be allowed to return before he was fit again to face the situation. In this way Elijah learned that God at least was in no way embarrassed by his nervous breakdown. God was still the same loving, caring, unperturbed God as He had ever been. God was so much in control of things in Israel that He could well afford to send Elijah away like this. Indeed, God is always so much in control of His business that He can always give His workers the holiday they need.

It was not only firmness God showed with Elijah, but also infinite tenderness and patience. Sometimes our friends, when they undergo great disappointments in life, give way like Job to the temptation to behave wildly and to talk bitterly about God. This mood may go on for so long that we become impatient with them. Perhaps we give them up. But in the Bible God deals gently, almost compassionately, with those who allow themselves to get into moods of depression and to give vent to wild talk. In the case of Elijah God had to wait for over forty days before He could do anything with him.

First of all God let Elijah sleep: 'He giveth his beloved sleep.'[2] Then when Elijah awoke, he found that a meal had been prepared for him by one of God's angels. How sensible and practical is the love of God! It reminds us of Jesus, who, after He awoke Jairus's daughter, told her parents to give her

[1] Isa. 49.4   [2] Ps. 127.2

something to eat,[1] and who at the Sea of Galilee had breakfast ready for His tired and frustrated disciples.[2] God's love is not concerned only about men's eternal salvation, but is also tender enough to sense their ordinary physical needs. Then God called Elijah to take an extended holiday and go apart from the world into retreat for He had something He wanted to say to him when he became more rested in body and soul. All this to a man who was in a petulant, rebellious mood! Through it all God was seeking to get Elijah into an attitude of mind in which He could give him a clearer understanding of what had been happening to him and to his people. Moreover, God had a fresh task about which he wanted to speak to Elijah when he was ready.

Time worked the desired change in Elijah's mood. He arrived at Mount Horeb, the mount on which God had spoken to Moses. Perhaps he wondered why he had been led there. Perhaps his mind was subdued by dwelling on the wonderful history of God's gracious dealings with His people in the midst of the wilderness through which he had to journey. When he arrived at Horeb Elijah was led to a cave. Perhaps this was the cave in which God had given to Moses the vision of His glory when He hid him in the cleft of the rock.

Then Elijah was tested to see what was in his heart and mind. '*What doest thou here, Elijah?*' God asked. He meant Elijah to express what he was feeling and thinking about. Elijah told God simply about his hard experience of defeat at Carmel, '*And he said, I have been very jealous for the Lord God of hosts: for the children of Israel have forsaken thy covenant, thrown down thine altars, and slain thy prophets with the sword; and I, even I only, am left; and they seek my life, to take it away*'.

There is now no note of bitterness in Elijah's attitude, no despairing prayer that he might die. The gentle treatment that God had given His servant had succeeded. It was now time for God to speak.

'*Go forth, and stand upon the mount before the Lord*,' was God's command to Elijah. '*And, behold, the Lord passed by, and a great and strong wind rent the mountains, and brake in pieces the rocks before the Lord; but the Lord was not in the wind: and after the wind an earthquake; but the Lord was not in the earthquake: and after the*

---

[1] Mark 5.43   [2] John 21.9

earthquake a fire; but the Lord was not in the fire: and after the fire a still small voice. And it was so, when Elijah heard it, that he wrapped his face in his mantle, and went out, and stood in the entering in of the cave.'

God was different from what he thought! The Lord was in '*the still small voice*' (or, as it should be translated, '*the sound of a gentle stillness*'). Elijah felt the presence of God in the stillness so near and so real that a fear and wonder came over his soul and he covered his face in reverence. Neither the whirlwind that rent the side of the mountains, nor the earthquake that seemed to shake the foundations of the earth, nor the fire that fell from the heavens, splendid and marvellous, forced Elijah to his knees in worship. These things did not convince his soul. It was the awe of the stillness that overwhelmed the man and made him cover his face as if he were afraid to look upon the glory of God.

God is teaching Elijah that He can pass by the earthquake and wind and fire, and still remain the Lord. He has the power to bring awe and conviction to the souls of men even without these vivid and spectacular signs of His omnipotence and fury and victory. Even if at times He sends earthquakes and thunderbolts to do His work, He remains the Lord in His power to manifest Himself and work wonders in the human heart long after these spectacular things have subsided in failure, and there are no visible signs left of His presence among men. After his experience at Mount Carmel Elijah had tended to identify the presence of God in Israel with the presence of the fire from heaven, and the victory of God with spectacular success. Here at Horeb he was in the place where God had revealed Himself to Moses and Israel through fire and earthquake. How much he was in need of this fresh lesson that God's power and victory and presence are never tied up with the spectacular and glorious happenings that unbelieving men long to cling to as their proof of God.

It is as important for us as it was for Elijah, to learn the same lesson. Many of us are apt to lay too much stress on the importance of our own vigorous and showy activity in advancing the Kingdom of God. We are apt to believe that blustering and spectacular ways of doing things are really more effective than ways that are less outwardly impressive. We are prone to believe in the whirlwind, the earthquake and the fire when we set about advancing the Kingdom of God and doing His work among men. Moreover, we tend to think that God is not there in our midst working mightily unless we see things happening on a large and visible scale. We long for spectacular and convulsive signs that God is at hand with His mighty revolutionary energy.

God does, of course, make concessions to our human longing for the visible and spectacular signs of His Kingdom. Out of His mercy and kindness to us God *can and does* use at times such spectacular and blustering methods as we are apt to want Him to use. He used the whirlwind and the earthquake and fire when He used Elijah at Carmel. He *can and does* use our publicity campaigns, our catchy methods, our techniques in mass evangelism. And the New Testament undoubtedly speaks of the Kingdom as finally breaking in upon this world in the midst of upheavals and signs that involve the whole earth in wonder and fear.

But while all this is true He wants us always to know that sometimes He prefers to be in the sound of a gentle stillness. He wants us to remember that at Horeb He was not in the earthquake or the wind or the fire. The manner of the coming of the Lord's Kingdom is not the manner of the coming of this world's kingdoms. The Lord does not necessarily herald the progress of His Kingdom with noise and the clash of arms or with spectacularly successful Church efforts or even with the establishment of great and lasting civilisations. He does not announce His victories immediately after they happen. He works greatly often through the silent and small and the insignificant. The Lord is in no turbulent hurry to prove that He is God. He gives man time to repent.

It was in order that He might impress this truth upon men that Jesus Christ never attempted to put on a grand show. Nor did He advertise Himself loudly, nor push His claims, nor use pomp and display. He offered nothing more convincing to prove the presence of God than the truth of His Word and the love which He showed in His person.

This passage may be meant to give some comfort to those who in the service of Christ have seen no whirlwind success following their efforts, who after much zeal and toil have failed to produce any convulsive revolution either in the Church or in society. Sometimes we are apt to be despondent when such is the case with us—especially when we see that elsewhere others can still produce mighty and spectacular evidences of God's working on a massive scale. We need not be jealous or disparaging. Such success can and may be a sign that God is indeed vigorously at work. Yet we need not take it too much to heart if our lot is different. After the earthquake and the fire had subsided the Lord was in the still small voice! In the midst of our success we are too often confronted by failure, and in the midst of our failures we are too often convinced of success, that we should either become too carried away by success or cast down by failure.

Back to Work and to Fellowship

God's final word to Elijah at Horeb was a summons to get back to work and back amongst the people of God. His task was to anoint Hazael as King of Syria, Jehu as future King of Israel, and Elisha as his own successor. God had a long-term plan of action involving each of these three. Each had his part to play in the events that would ultimately lead to the ruin of the house of Ahab. To have been given such a task must have meant a great deal of encouragement for Elijah. Things to him had seemed chaotic since the glorious day of the attempted revolution at Carmel. But he knew now that God's plan of action was still clearly defined. It was to be different from what he had imagined. God was now going to involve such seemingly pagan and wild characters as Hazael and Jehu in the business which up to now He had so exclusively shared with Elijah. But what He had promised was surely to happen, and Elijah had still to play his own part.

The realisation that there was work to do and that he could still be of use no doubt helped Elijah himself to recover from his breakdown. There is a biblical basis for the advice we sometimes give to despondent people that they should take up some worthwhile Christian service even as a means to cure despondency! Being given a task to do can help to steady a man's faith and to deliver him from gloom.

But of more importance still was the Lord's advice to Elijah to seek out the hidden Church and to enter its fellowship.

ELIJAH'S FLIGHT

'*Yet have I left me seven thousand in Israel, all the knees which have not bowed unto Baal, and every mouth which hath not kissed him.*' Elijah's complaint had been that he had felt overwhelmingly alone in bearing his witness to God. This had been perhaps the hardest part of his burden as a prophet. God now tells him that he need no longer go on bearing this burden alone. He can now go back and seek out from among the people of the land those who like himself have refused to compromise with Baal. He will find now that they are more numerous than he has imagined. In such fellowship he will find strength and courage and further healing for his depression of mind and heart.

God has made us so that the cure for most of our spiritual ailments can be given to us only if we take our humble place at the feet of others in the fellowship of His Church. Sometimes it is true that men are involved, as Elijah has hitherto been involved, in necessarily bearing a great burden of loneliness in the service of Christ. But there is a limit to the amount of isolation that any man can bear—or is expected to bear. And it becomes tragedy indeed when men for no other reasons than spiritual pride and self-centred habit and suspicion of the sincerity of others who profess Christ, refuse to turn to the fellowship of the Church for the strength that God wants to give them within it. Even great and lonely Elijah had to submit in the last resort to the word that reminded him that it was only by regarding himself as a part of a great and invincible Church that he could become a finally courageous and victorious servant of God. None of us is stronger than he was, and none of us apart from the fellowship of the Church is likely to do any better than to end up permanently sulking under the juniper tree.

POSTSCRIPT

Martin Buber, a great Jewish philosopher, in an essay entitled 'Biblical Leadership' points out that, whereas history, as the world writes it, glorifies success, the Bible glorifies men who have failed. In ordinary history books the successful men are regarded as the important ones. 'History,' he says, 'croons a low dirge over the overpowered heroes, but loud does its paean ring . . . for those who are crowned with success.'

But then he points out that the Bible looks on things quite differently. 'The Bible knows nothing of this intrinsic worth of success. On the contrary, when it announces a successful deed, it is in duty bound to announce with utmost detail the failure involved in the success.'

All the great leaders of the Bible, according to the Biblical story, failed to accomplish their task. The history of Moses is one of only partial success, thwarted continually by defeat, failure and frustration. The history of David can be summed up in exactly the same sentence. 'And,' says Buber, 'this glorification of failure culminates in the long line of prophets whose existence is plain failure. They live in failure; failure is the breath of their nostrils, it is for them to fight and not to conquer.' Here is Elijah learning in the same school of failure.

We can understand Elijah's experience better than he understood it himself. In Jesus Christ we have seen the powers of evil defeated once for all through His triumph in His Cross and Resurrection. In that final conflict in which Jesus, God's own Son, defeated the powers of evil He fought no weak enemy, no easy battle. He Himself overcame only through suffering apparent defeat and utter humiliation. His agony and bloody sweat, His fearful hours upon the Cross in which He had to pour forth all His strength in order to win the conflict, show us that here in the conflict with evil we are up against a tragic and terrible mystery of a power greater than all human power, yet overcome by God in human flesh and to be overcome only by those who range themselves on His side in the conflict. It was in this battle with evil that Elijah was taking part in his day and generation. That is why he suffered victory in defeat and defeat in victory.

Evil has been defeated finally and for ever by Jesus Christ. The course of the battle has been turned decisively towards an inevitable and complete victory which shall be manifested when Christ shall come again. Yet the battle still goes on and we are in it. We all know only too well that we have to fight evil within our own hearts and in the world around us. And in this fight evil still has the power to rally its forces and put on an apparent show of triumph. We have to watch and pray. We may find ourselves having to cope with situations that will seem even desperate, if we take our eyes off the hope of His coming. Our battles with evil will have the same character of hardness as that of Elijah. We, too, will be brought into the same humiliating situations. Certainly we will overcome. We will share in the experience of Paul, who called his life a constant pageant of triumph through Jesus Christ. But, in the midst of this triumph, we will share in the disappointments, the frustrations, and even, paradoxically, in the failures which it has been the lot of the people to suffer in every generation. For we have to learn as Elijah did that we have to be made conformable not only to the Resurrection of Jesus Christ but also to His death.

THE CALL OF ELISHA

So he departed thence, and found Elisha the son of Shaphat, who was plowing with twelve yoke of oxen before him, and he with the twelfth: and Elijah passed by him, and cast his mantle upon him. And he left the oxen, and ran after Elijah, and said, Let me, I pray thee, kiss my father and my mother, and then I will follow thee. And he said unto him, Go back again: for what have I done to thee? And he returned back from him, and took a yoke of oxen, and slew them, and boiled their flesh with the instruments of the oxen, and gave unto the people, and they did eat. Then he arose, and went after Elijah, and ministered unto him.

I KINGS 19.19-21

THE 'HOUR OF DECISION'

This might be called the 'hour of decision' in Elisha's life. We see him in the field at Abel Meholah. They are ploughing. Twelve ploughs are at work, and Elisha's is the twelfth. He comes last because he is the son of the master, following upon the servants in what is obviously an important and wealthy estate. They are no doubt thankful that this year the rain has come at last after three years' drought, and has made it worth while to plough the ground. They are probably talking about the famine and its effects on the people and on the land. They go on to discuss Elijah the Tishbite and the great day at Carmel when Elijah had both Jezebel and Ahab trembling for their lives. But Elijah has disappeared since then and they wonder where he has gone to hide, and why he should have fled after such a great day's victory.

Suddenly the gaunt figure who had so captured their imagination and whom they all immediately recognise is seen striding across the fields. He pauses as he approaches to look round for his man, and then he goes right up to accost Elisha. He takes off his mantle and lays it on the shoulders of the young man as he is ploughing. Nothing is said. Nothing requires to be said. The act of Elijah carries its own and obvious significance. Elisha knows what is meant and the onlookers know what is meant. It is a call to leave everything and follow

Elijah so that he can succeed him when his work is finished. It is a call to prepare himself from now on to step into Elijah's office when he is taken away by God, to take up where Elijah leaves off the struggle against the evils that threaten the nation. It is a call to follow here and now, and to submit himself to training for the task. He must become the companion of the man he is to succeed in order that he may become more fitted to be his successor. So pressing and urgent is this call that he must decide here and now without delay even while he is in the field.

This is a day and an hour Elisha will remember and look back upon as more filled with significance than any other day or hour in his life. It is a day and an hour when not only his career but indeed his destiny seems to be decided—decided by God and yet at the same time decided by his own free choice.

The story of Elijah's call to Elisha is very like the stories we find in the Gospels of the calls which Jesus gave to men as He preached and journeyed throughout Galilee—especially the call to Peter and James and John as they were mending their nets[1] and He passed by and called on them to leave all and follow Him, and the call to Matthew when he was seated at the receipt of custom.[2]

In the same way Jesus Christ is always challenging us to yield our lives to Him today, and in a true sense every day is a day of decision. Yet there are days when the living Christ seems to come near to us in a specially significant way and to challenge us with particularly decisive urgency—as Elijah challenged Elisha on that historic day of their encounter in the field. He seems to come specially near to us in order that we may be brought to the point of a pressing decision as to whether or not we will have His forgiveness and His blessing, and as to whether or not we are going to redirect our lives to His service.

For many of us this hour of decision is experienced within the fellowship of the Church. As we listen to the Word of God, somehow or other, in a way we cannot explain, the living Christ comes near to us and presses His claim upon us. We find ourselves sitting not at the feet of a minister preaching, but

[1] Matt. 4.21   [2] Matt. 9.9

at the feet of our Lord Himself ready to open up His heart to us. Such hours can be quite unforgettable and quite decisive for all the rest of our lives. The Apostle John in his Gospel seldom records the time of day when anything happened, but when he describes the very first interview which he and his brother James had with Jesus in His house he records the time of day at which it all happened, as if he wants us to realise that that hour was for him of decisive and far-reaching significance and of the most precious memory. 'It was about the tenth hour,'[1] he says.

IT IS GOD'S DECISION THAT MAKES OUR DECISION POSSIBLE

The emphasis in this story is on the fact that it was God who had chosen Elisha and that it was God who had taken all the initiative in forcing this decision. Elisha was chosen by God for this task some time before he was called to it by Elijah. It was some weeks previously when Elijah was at Horeb that God told him to search out and find Elisha and anoint him as his successor. God had decided all this even before Elisha was given the opportunity of deciding. Elijah's task as he came to anoint him was not first of all to ask him if he was willing to accept the office or to appeal for his help, but merely to announce a decision that God had already made about him. Elisha was invested with the sign of his prophetic office before he was consulted about his willingness to respond.

As far as Elisha's first reaction is concerned there is no sign here that he had been preparing himself for this call or this task. It is probable that he would never have chosen it of his own free will or voluntarily thrust himself forward into it. There is no suggestion that he had secret dreams in his heart of fulfilling such a position in Israel. He seems taken aback and unprepared in mind and attitude. This hour of decision had come not because Elisha was emotionally and mentally ripe for such a decision, but because God's word and God's call had been announced.

Moreover, Elisha felt not only that God had decided about him, but also that God was there at that moment personally confronting him and challenging him through Elijah's strange action. Elisha felt that he was facing not simply God's

---

[1] John 1.39

messenger but God Himself, that he was listening not simply to a decree God made at Horeb a week or two previously but to the living voice of God calling him to yield his life there and then. When the mantle was cast upon him he felt an overwhelming constraint and undeniable urge within himself to give himself from then on to the living God. He felt that something had happened to him that had made his future different from that moment. God was there seeking entrance into his life in a new way in order to compel him to choose to take up this task. So powerful and real was the constraint he felt to follow the call he had heard that he was in doubt even if it was right for him to go back home and kiss his father and mother good-bye.

This then was the hour of *God's* decision about Elisha. It was the hour when God Himself pressed that decision upon His servant. Yet it was also the hour of Elisha's decision about God. In spite of the fact that Elisha felt that he was thus predestined and inwardly constrained to follow Elijah, there is no doubt that there in the field at Abel Meholah on that day he himself had to make a real hard and crucial decision as to whether or not he was going to respond to Elijah's call. Even though God had decided for him Elisha felt he must decide. He must respond with a freely given and a freely spoken 'I will' to God's 'thou shalt'. That is why he was at first so obviously disturbed. He wanted to decide rightly what he must do. He knew that it was of vital and urgent importance that he should decide. Obviously it was a costly decision to have to make. It meant giving up his home and wealth and his settled life. Obviously he counted the cost and weighed up the sacrifice involved. He faced the possibility of being able to say 'no' to God's call. He shuddered at the possibility, and put it away from him with deliberate effort in saying 'yes'. Even though he was predestined and constrained inwardly, he was nevertheless fully responsible in the decision he had to make.

When we are ourselves faced with making any 'decision for Christ' we must remember that it is only Jesus Christ's initiative and Jesus Christ's decision to come and challenge and call us that makes it possible for us to 'decide' for Him. Always His love for us and His decision for us precede our love for Him. We cannot love Him before He first loves us. We cannot decide for Him unless He first decides to come to us and call us. Bartimaeus sat by the roadside begging day after day. He had no doubt heard of Jesus' power to heal, and he no doubt prayed that God would bring the Master his way. But he could make no other decision about this till one day he asked what the noise on the road meant, and he was told, 'Jesus of Nazareth passeth by'.[1] Then was indeed his hour of decision. It was his hour of decision because Jesus had decided about him and was there challenging him as if to offer him sight. Yet Bartimaeus had to decide there and then in a most determined way. It was now or never if he was to grasp Jesus Christ and have His forgiveness and His healing. Bartimaeus was on his feet without any delay crying, 'Jesus, thou Son of David, have mercy on me'.

It is the same with us. We know that when Jesus confronts us in His grace we have to decide. We know that we must choose God if we are to have God. We must seek God if we are to find God. We must lay hold of what Christ holds out to us if it is to be ours. But we know with equal and utter certainty that when we find ourselves on the right side in the battle of life, enriched beyond all our dreams with what we have found and what we have grasped in grasping Jesus Christ, that it was not we who chose, but rather He who chose us, it was not we who found Him, but rather He who found us. It is not on our hold of Christ that our salvation depends, but on His hold of us. It is not we who have decided about Him, but He who has decided about us.

ELIJAH SETS ELISHA FREE

From the brevity of the account of the conversation that took place after Elisha made his great decision it is difficult for anyone to define precisely what their words meant, but for our purpose in interpreting the incident today we can assume that these men had the same doubts and difficulties as men have today when they are confronted by the claims of God. Many questions must have burned in Elisha's mind. We hear him asking only one of them, and we hear Elijah's answer in words so pregnant and full of such practical wisdom that we

[1] Luke 18.37

wish we had more of the teaching of Elijah recorded in the Bible.

Elisha's problem was whether he should return home to kiss his father and mother farewell. He knew that this call of God must be put before the claim of family affection, but, acting under his first impulse, he wondered whether he must now go much further. Should he allow human affection to have any claim at all on him now? Dare he linger even a moment now in his home farm while Elijah was striding on before him in the direction of the hills? He knew that Elijah was a man without home, without personal friend, without much time for domestic trivialities and polite talk. Did this call mean that from now on, he Elisha, had to become a man like Elijah, grim, distant, unbending? Should he from now on deny much of what had been most human in his nature? He felt at least that he was bound to ask Elijah to decide for him.

It was with a mind perplexed with such thoughts that '*he left the oxen, and ran after Elijah, and said, Let me, I pray thee, kiss my father and my mother, and then I will follow thee. And he said unto him, Go back again: for what have I done to thee?*'

'*Go back again,*' said Elijah. It was an appeal to Elisha to be moderate and sensible and human in his judgment about what God was requiring of him at that moment and at that period in his service of God. There was no need for him to imagine that God meant him to be so foolish as to try to deny the expression of his natural affection at that great moment in his life.

H. R. Mackintosh, a great and wise teacher, once said to his class: 'Gentlemen, after a man is converted, he has sometimes to be made into a human being again—and sometimes it takes a year or two for that to happen.' It sometimes happens that when men have undergone a great and deep religious experience, in the enthusiasm and wholeheartedness of their first response, and in their desire to express the radical nature of the change that has come over them, they tend to go to extremes of rigour and self-discipline, and are tempted to act inhumanly and unnaturally where there is no need for it. In the Middle Ages sometimes men newly initiated in the monastic orders would take up their religious discipline and fasting and scourging with such thoroughness as almost to kill themselves.

Today sometimes enthusiastic young people in their very keenness to give expression to the call they have heard from Jesus Christ will needlessly grieve parents and friends by the distant nature of the new attitude they take up to former companions and dear ones, and while cutting out evil things from their lives will sometimes unnecessarily also cut out much that may be good and natural and humanising.

Elijah's word to Elisha, '*Go back again*'—go and be sensible and human!—enabled the younger man to see things in their true proportions again, and to act more naturally than he had at first intended. He said farewell from that day to his home and his farm. But he said farewell in a way that made it a day of rejoicing for his home rather than a day of gloom and tension, a day to be remembered rather than a day to be forgotten. He made a feast. He perhaps spoke to them of the call he had heard, of what he felt this call would involve. He took his departure in full recognition of and gratitude for what his home had made him.

Elijah had a further word for Elisha before he left him: '*What have I done to thee?*' He may have felt that there was a real danger that Elisha might make him, as the one through whom his call had come to him, too important and dominating an influence in his life. Here was Elisha beginning to ask him for decisions about what he had to do. But how could he, Elijah, even begin to think or make decisions for a man so different from himself, a man he knew so little about. '*What have I done to thee?*'

In saying this Elijah took up the only healthy attitude that a good Christian leader of men can take up towards those who may come under his influence. Every man must ultimately make his own judgment on moral questions and on practical issues. It is an evil thing when any man of strong influence or personality so dominates others that they no longer need to make their own decisions by themselves at the feet of Jesus Christ. The minister, the Church, the group can give advice, but each man must decide as if he stood before Christ alone. And when one man finds that his influence is so dominating that another man is not thinking for himself, or when he finds that he is being set up as a standard to live by and as a giver of laws, then it is time for him to say clearly to other men,

THE CALL OF ELISHA

'*What have I done to thee*,' and to point them from himself to Jesus Christ.

Paul's great words to the Corinthians when he called to them to stop being dominated by either Paul or Apollos or Cephas, in order to allow themselves to be dominated by Jesus Christ alone, deserve to be quoted here. 'Who then is Paul, and who is Apollos, but ministers by whom ye believed. . . . So then neither is he that planteth any thing, neither he that watereth; but God that giveth the increase. . . . Therefore let no man glory in men. For all things are yours; whether Paul, or Apollos, or Cephas, or the world, or life, or death, or things present, or things to come; all are yours; And ye are Christ's; and Christ is God's.'[1]

Our Lord Himself alone has the right to dominate other men and to decide for other men in every issue that faces them. His will for us must be our will. And in His claims upon men He always demands the submission of our whole will and thought and affection and conscience. We must have no independence of judgment when we deal with Jesus Christ. And yet even our Lord Himself does not dominate us through laying down laws for us or hard and fast rules of conduct. He gives us His friendship and leaves us with wonderful and yet terrifying freedom often to judge for ourselves under the gentle yet compelling influence of His Spirit and presence. Did he not say to His disciples, 'Henceforth I call you not servants; for the servant knoweth not what his lord doeth: but I have called you friends; for all things that I have heard of my Father I have made known unto you'?[2]

[1] 1 Cor. 3.5-7, 21-3   [2] John 15.15

NABOTH'S VINEYARD

And it came to pass after these things, that Naboth the Jezreelite had a vineyard, which was in Jezreel, hard by the palace of Ahab king of Samaria. And Ahab spake unto Naboth, saying, Give me thy vineyard, that I may have it for a garden of herbs, because it is near unto my house: and I will give thee for it a better vineyard than it; or, if it seem good to thee, I will give thee the worth of it in money. And Naboth said to Ahab, The Lord forbid it me, that I should give the inheritance of my fathers unto thee. And Ahab came into his house heavy and displeased because of the word which Naboth the Jezreelite had spoken to him: for he had said, I will not give thee the inheritance of my fathers. And he laid him down upon his bed, and turned away his face, and would eat no bread. But Jezebel his wife came to him, and said unto him, Why is thy spirit so sad, that thou eatest no bread? And he said unto her, Because I spake unto Naboth the Jezreelite, and said unto him, Give me thy vineyard for money; or else, if it please thee, I will give thee another vineyard for it: and he answered, I will not give thee my vineyard. And Jezebel his wife said unto him, Dost thou now govern the kingdom of Israel? arise, and eat bread, and let thine heart be merry: I will give thee the vineyard of Naboth the Jezreelite. So she wrote letters in Ahab's name, and sealed them with his seal, and sent the letters unto the elders and to the nobles that were in his city, dwelling with Naboth. And she wrote in the letters, saying, Proclaim a fast, and set Naboth on high among the people: and set two men, sons of Belial, before him, to bear witness against him, saying, Thou didst blaspheme God and the king. And then carry him out, and stone him, that he may die. And the men of his city, even the elders and the nobles who were the inhabitants in his city, did as Jezebel had sent unto them, and as it was written in the letters which she had sent unto them. They proclaimed a fast, and set Naboth on high among the people. And there came in two men, children of Belial, and sat before him: and the men of Belial witnessed against him, even against Naboth, in the presence of the people, saying, Naboth did blaspheme God and the king. Then they carried him forth out of the city, and stoned him with stones, that he died. Then they sent to Jezebel, saying, Naboth is stoned, and is dead. And it came to pass, when Jezebel heard that Naboth was stoned, and was dead, that Jezebel said to Ahab, Arise, take possession of the vineyard of Naboth the Jezreelite, which he refused to give thee for money: for Naboth is not alive, but dead. And it came to pass, when Ahab heard that Naboth was dead, that Ahab rose up to go down to the vineyard of Naboth the

NABOTH'S VINEYARD 63

Jezreelite, to take possession of it. And the word of the Lord came to Elijah the Tishbite, saying, Arise, go down to meet Ahab king of Israel, which is in Samaria: behold, he is in the vineyard of Naboth, whither he is gone down to possess it. And thou shalt speak unto him, saying, Thus saith the Lord, Hast thou killed, and also taken possession? And thou shalt speak unto him, saying, Thus saith the Lord, In the place where dogs licked the blood of Naboth shall dogs lick thy blood, even thine. And Ahab said to Elijah, Hast thou found me, O mine enemy? And he answered, I have found thee: because thou hast sold thyself to work evil in the sight of the Lord.

I KINGS 21.1-20

Queen Jezebel was angry. She had been angry about many things since she married Ahab, king of Israel. She had been angry about the size of the palace he gave her, for in her father's country of Tyre they had palaces that were palaces indeed! She was angry at the size of the garden round the palace. She had not enough room to grow her favourite herbs. She felt in fact that the whole situation of the royal family in this backward land required radical improvement.

One person who annoyed her was Naboth, her next-door neighbour. He had a vineyard hard by her palace. When she went to her window to look at the view her eyes sometimes met his, staring towards her in a way no one should dream of staring at royalty. When she wanted quietness she heard him pruning his vines noisily, and her siesta was often disturbed.

She determined to stop all this Israelite nonsense. She was going to have Naboth's vineyard. Superficially this seemed a harmless enough desire. Let Ahab go and offer Naboth a good price for his land, or let him have another vineyard in place of his present one. Who could object to such a fair and square business proposal? But even to make such a proposal was a violation of something regarded as good and sacred in Israel. It meant trampling on ancient customs that had strong religious sanctions. 'The land shall not be sold for ever: for the land is mine,'[1] said their law. Land therefore was considered as given by God to the people, and it was cutting across the sacred bonds of the nation's unity and family life for a man to sell his land, or for another, even the king, to

[1] Lev. 25.23

offer to purchase it from him. The whole religious and legal tradition of Israel was against anyone, even the king, acquiring lands or great estates. For Ahab to go to Naboth and suggest the sale of his vineyard was a mean and unworthy errand for a king to undertake.

But what could Ahab do? He could not go and explain all this to Jezebel, that it was against the law of God for a man to sell his inheritance. She would not understand that Israel was a peculiar nation that had God especially near to them. She would not believe that there was no nation that had customs, statutes and judgments so righteous as the law of Israel. He could not make her see that the laws of Israel were not given to suit the greed of kings, as in her father's kingdom in Tyre, but were given by God for the good of the people, and for His eternal purposes. Whenever he had spoken about God's promises to Abraham and Moses, and had tried to explain all this, she always gave the same reply, '*Dost thou now govern the kingdom of Israel?*'—'Are you a king or a puppet?'

All this involved Ahab in a fearful conflict of mind and heart. He knew well the traditions of his own people, and he had enough respect for them to have a bad conscience at breaking them. But he had married Jezebel. He had given her his affection. He had come under her influence to such an extent that he had now no power to assert his own will against hers. Therefore we are not surprised to see him soon walking down to Naboth's house, on the most degrading mission that any man could undertake. He had been sent by Jezebel to propose to this honest and God-fearing neighbour that they should join hands in something that was bound to be against his conscience. Of course Ahab put it smoothly and politely, almost humbly. He tried to bribe Naboth with the good prospects that the sin would hold: '*I will give thee for it a better vineyard than it; or . . . the worth of it in money.*'

Naboth rebuked Ahab with as noble an answer as any commoner ever gave a king: '*The Lord forbid it me, that I should give the inheritance of my fathers unto thee.*' The answer reminded Ahab of the reality of the God he had forsaken. It reminded him that though the name of the Lord meant nothing to himself, nevertheless there were others who had proved His reality and who feared Him. No doubt God was trying to speak to Ahab through the rebuke that Naboth gave him in his vineyard. It was the voice of God Himself that Ahab heard as Naboth spoke. Therefore it was Ahab's opportunity to repent. He could now choose whether the rebuke of Naboth was going to make him completely rethink his position and alter his life. There is a 'godly sorrow', says Paul, which 'worketh repentance', but there is also a 'sorrow of the world' which 'worketh death'.[1] At that moment Ahab could choose which kind of sorrow the rebuke of Naboth was to bring to his heart—the sorrow of true repentance over the fact that he had indeed sinned against the love of God, or mere bitterness and selfish regret over the humiliation he had received.

Ahab was certainly stricken with great sorrow. He went home '*heavy*' of heart, and sore '*displeased*'. Certainly he deeply regretted the course of life that had brought him into the desperate position of being a miserable tool in the hands of Jezebel and a wretched object of scorn among his own people. He went to bed, '*turned away his face, and would eat no bread*'.

But instead of allowing this experience to be the birth pangs of a new life of repentance, Ahab allowed it to drive him more under the power of Jezebel than ever before. It is said that William Rufus had a picture of God on one side of his shield and a picture of the Devil on the other, with the motto underneath, 'Ready for either'. Ahab gives us a truer picture of the man who compromises. He was ready for neither. He had no answer for Naboth. He could not stand before his face. But neither could he withstand Jezebel. When she entered the room and found him sulking she taunted him about his weakness and stupidity. He had to yield himself now, submissive, into her hands. He was beaten and she could do what she liked. Jezebel took the situation under control. She applied in Israel the ways of the king of Tyre. She knew enough of Israelite law to be aware that kings fell heir to all lands confiscated through treason and blasphemy. Her plan was to have Naboth so accused. She wrote the fatal letters, executed the plot, and within a few weeks Naboth was dead and his lands belonged to the king. And the order came to Ahab from her: '*Arise, take possession of the vineyard of Naboth*

---

[1] 2 Cor. 7.10

the Jezreelite, which he refused to give thee for money: for Naboth is not alive, but dead.'

It seems when we read this story that God had failed to watch over Naboth. Murder and perjury and blasphemy had been committed, and God had done nothing. But God was watching the situation in Israel nevertheless. As Ahab stood in the midst of the vineyard surveying the property, planning the layout of his new garden, a voice arrested him: '*Hast thou killed, and also taken possession?*' In the eyes of God it was not only Jezebel that had murdered Naboth, it was Ahab. In the eyes of God we are guilty for the sins in which we are involved through our weakness, and carelessness, and consent, as though we had committed them with deliberate hand.

A WARNING TO THE NATION

This story shows us how sinister and terrible is the havoc that can be worked in the midst of a nation when true religion becomes neglected. Ahab and Jezebel, on the throne of Israel, stand for the fact that the people of Israel as a whole had lost their sense of God. They had lost touch with the true faith of their forefathers. They neglected to consider the true meaning of their law. They accepted Jezebel and her ways because they had no sense of the reality of the living God in their midst.

Naboth in the story stands for something too. He was a free Israelite. Because the people of Israel had a tradition of faith in the Lord and had for generations accepted and honoured His holy law, they had enjoyed a measure of security and freedom for the individual in their midst that none of the surrounding nations knew anything about. In Israel the ordinary man enjoyed protection in his fields and in his home because he belonged to a people who acknowledge God. Naboth, then, stands for the simple honest man who depends upon the liberties and rights which a living faith in God can preserve within a community.

And this story tells us plainly that when people neglect God's law and lose their sense of God, then ordinary men like Naboth begin to lose their rights and liberties. It warns us that when a nation begins to think, as Israel did in the time of Jezebel, that a profitable alliance with evil is more important than to stand by the godly traditions of their past, then the first casualty is the liberty of the subject. It was Naboth, the ordinary man who depended upon faith and justice, who was crushed when the nation lost its fear of God.

This incident then reminds us of the warning uttered in the Book of Proverbs: 'Where there is no vision, the people perish.'[1] Loss of 'vision' within a nation is simply loss of a sense of God. This took place in Israel gradually and yet surely as each generation allowed its religious life and religious thought and practice to become more and more corrupted by falsehood. The incident reminds us too of the great affirmation of the Apostle Paul about liberty: 'Where the Spirit of the Lord is, there is liberty.'[2] We make a profound mistake when we imagine that political liberty is something that is won and kept only by political and economic forces and methods. The true political liberty which can bring security and satisfaction to the free individual in the midst of a free community is the gift of the Spirit of God, and it can be fostered and kept within a nation only as men allow the true and living God who has revealed Himself in Jesus Christ to be proclaimed and worshipped without hindrance or neglect.

A WARNING TO THE INDIVIDUAL

The story shows us how sinister and terrible is the havoc worked by evil not only in the midst of Israel but also in the personal life of Ahab, through his allowing the influence of Jezebel, her culture and her religion, to dominate his life. It shows the harvest of bitterness and sorrow that he reaped, and the depth of degradation and shame into which he was plunged, almost against his own will and judgment, through the decision he made when he married her and put himself under her power. Ahab is spoken of in this chapter as a man who, in making a common cause with Jezebel in sin, has '*sold himself to work evil in the sight of the Lord*', and in an earlier chapter it is clearly stated that his marriage with Jezebel was the one sin which displeased God more than anything else he did in his life. Ahab's murder of Naboth illustrates the working out of the consequences of his '*selling himself*' through his marriage to work whatever evil was the will of Jezebel.

We feel pity for Ahab as we read all this. He was obviously

[1] Prov. 29.18 [2] 2 Cor. 3.17

a man in the grip of an evil power stronger than himself and he could not regain any freedom. Yet we must frankly recognise the fact that Ahab himself was responsible through his own deliberate choice of giving himself over to the evil influence which dominated him. He himself made the choice as a result of which his life was so determined by evil.

The story is a warning to us all of how far our, at first, apparently innocent relationship with any kind of evil influence can ultimately lead us even against our will if we allow it more and more to fascinate, allure and grip us. We know only too well from our own observation and experience that this Ahab and Jezebel story is constantly being re-enacted in ordinary life. One evil man can so dominate and influence others of weaker character that they descend to depths of evil doing and thinking to which by themselves they could never have sunk. We know too that an individual can often allow himself to be led on by a gang or group to commit an evil that would be quite abhorrent to his own better judgment.

But we are reminded in the story of something even more sinister than this. All those forms of human bondage whereby one man can become '*sold to work evil*', as Ahab was, are, according to the New Testament, merely the sign that there is a power greater than human into whose hands men are 'sold under sin'[1] so that they have no power to choose the good they might even wish to do. This is how the New Testament speaks of man's bondage apart from Jesus Christ. The man who does not have the liberty that is given to him by Christ is a man who is bound to live like Ahab, under the terrible bondage and domination of evil tendency. His life is dictated by 'the law of sin and death'[2] ruling in his members and his mind, a law from which he cannot go free. His destiny is determined by his master, sin, to whom he has sold himself to work evil, and whose wages are death itself.

This is how the New Testament speaks of the bondage in which men live apart from Jesus Christ. It was this bondage which Jesus warned Peter against when he said to him, 'Simon, Simon, behold, Satan hath desired to have you. . . .'[3] We do not like such language, for we would find it too depressing and too awful to take seriously the thought that those

---

[1] Rom. 7.14   [2] Rom. 8.2   [3] Luke 22.31

around us who do not have faith in Christ can really be living under such slavery.

And yet Paul reminds us that when we examine even our own Christian moral experience and take our own battle with evil seriously we can find ouselves involved in such a constant and bitter struggle with evil in our own hearts and our own circumstances that we are bound to take all this language about the power of evil to control human life with the utmost seriousness. Paul himself, even after he became a Christian, found that the struggle with the evil power within himself from which Christ had set him free was nevertheless hard and stern. He described his experience in unforgettable language in Romans, chapter seven: 'We know that the law is spiritual: but I am carnal, sold under sin.... For the good that I would I do not: but the evil which I would not, that I do.... O wretched man that I am! who shall deliver me from the body of this death? I thank God through Jesus Christ.'[1] If this is the Christian experience of an Apostle of Christ who has wakened up with new and glorious power to shake himself free from the bondage of the evil powers that dominate men in human life, how great indeed must be the reality of that bondage and the strength of the tyranny that binds men to work evil!

Yet in the face of this we can have the 'glorious liberty of the children of God'.[2] In the midst of our conflict we can cry with the utmost certainty and with full assurance of victory, 'I thank God through Jesus Christ!' It is against the background of the slavery and bondage of such as Ahab that we can understand what it really means when sinners find liberty and peace at the feet of Jesus Christ.

A WARNING OF JUDGMENT TO COME

One of the most dramatic parts of this story is the way in which Elijah appeared at the very moment when Ahab went down to take possession of the vineyard. God, through his prophet, had run His man to earth. He did not save Naboth, but He sought out his murderer with unerring justice. It is a mystery why God allows so many innocent men to die as Naboth did. We ask why, but we have no answer. Nevertheless

[1] Rom. 7.14, 19, 24-5   [2] Rom. 8.21

we know that God, even though He has to wait until the final day of judgment, will eventually run His man to earth.

'*Hast thou found me, O mine enemy?*' Ahab cried out in dismay when he found himself confronted by the dreaded presence of Elijah.

God is the One who finds men. He finds men in the depths of their iniquity. He finds the lost, even though they make their bed in Hell. He finds men in order either to free them and forgive them, or to judge them. Who knows, whether even at that late hour, Elijah might have been sent to save this man Ahab if, instead of calling God his enemy, he had decided from then on to call God his friend!

AHAZIAH AND ELIJAH

Then Moab rebelled against Israel after the death of Ahab. And Ahaziah fell down through a lattice in his upper chamber that was in Samaria, and was sick: and he sent messengers, and said unto them, Go, enquire of Baal-zebub the god of Ekron whether I shall recover of this disease. But the angel of the Lord said to Elijah the Tishbite, Arise, go up to meet the messengers of the king of Samaria, and say unto them, Is it not because there is not a god in Israel, that ye go to enquire of Baal-zebub the god of Ekron? Now therefore thus saith the Lord, Thou shalt not come down from that bed on which thou art gone up, but shalt surely die. And Elijah departed. And when the messengers turned back unto him, he said unto them, Why are ye now turned back? And they said unto him, There came a man up to meet us, and said unto us, Go, turn again unto the king that sent you, and say unto him, Thus saith the Lord, Is it not because there is not a God in Israel, that thou sendest to enquire of Baal-zebub the god of Ekron? therefore thou shalt not come down from that bed on which thou art gone up, but shalt surely die. And he said unto them, What manner of man was he which came up to meet you, and told you these words? And they answered him, He was an hairy man, and girt with a girdle of leather about his loins. And he said, It is Elijah the Tishbite. Then the king sent unto him a captain of fifty with his fifty. And he went up to him: and, behold, he sat on the top of an hill. And he spake unto him, Thou man of God, the king hath said, Come down. And Elijah answered and said to the captain of fifty, If I be a man of God, then let fire come down from heaven, and consume thee and thy fifty. And there came down fire from heaven, and consumed him and his fifty. Again also he sent unto him another captain of fifty with his fifty. And he answered and said unto him, O man of God, thus hath the king said, Come down quickly. And Elijah answered and said unto them, If I be a man of God, let fire come down from heaven, and consume thee and thy fifty. And the fire of God came down from heaven, and consumed him and his fifty. And he sent again a captain of the third fifty with his fifty. And the third captain of fifty went up, and came and fell on his knees before Elijah, and besought him, and said unto him, O man of God, I pray thee, let my life, and the life of these fifty thy servants, be precious in thy sight. Behold, there came fire down from heaven, and burnt up the two captains of the former fifties with their fifties: therefore let my life now be precious in thy sight. And the angel of the Lord said unto Elijah, Go down with him: be not afraid of him. And he arose, and went down with him unto the king.

And he said unto him, Thus saith the Lord, Forasmuch as thou hast sent messengers to enquire of Baal-zebub the god of Ekron, is it not because there is no God in Israel to enquire of his word? therefore thou shalt not come down off that bed on which thou art gone up, but shalt surely die. So he died according to the word of the Lord which Elijah had spoken.

2 KINGS 1.1-17

AHAZIAH BOUND AND YET FREE

When we first read about Ahaziah we are inclined merely to pity him, especially when we consider the circumstances under which he was born, the environment that surrounded him from his childhood, the disastrous times in which he succeeded to the throne, and the national and personal misfortunes that occurred shortly after his reign began.

He was the child of Ahab and Jezebel. If ever there should have been a problem child or a juvenile delinquent it was surely Ahaziah. Brought up by two such parents we should expect his mind to be perverted and his character warped.

Moreover, he faced serious political and economic trouble at the very moment he came to the throne. His father Ahab had had plenty of troubles to face at home, but at least during his reign he had managed to keep together the small Isrealite empire in a fairly secure condition. But on the death of Ahab and the accession of Ahaziah the King of Moab rebelled. Moab had been for years a vassal state to Israel, rendering a valuable annual contribution and held down by fear and force. The revolt of Moab was a significant reminder to those in power in Israel that they were not such a strong political force as once they had been. It was a reminder too that any state of affairs built up by force and fear is bound in the long run to disintegrate. It is a reminder to us today that loyalty based on force is bound ultimately to turn into rebellious reaction, whether in the sphere of political or of family relationships. Moab will always rebel against Israel.

Ahaziah's troubles after the rebellion of Moab were rendered more acute by a simple accident which occurred possibly, while the Moabite war was in progress. Ahaziah had seen his father killed in battle. He wanted to ensure his own safety, so he elected to remain in the comfort and security of his palace rather than risk the battlefield. But while he was leaning against a window in his house he fell through it. It was a most undignified experience for a king who might have been out among his troops in the battle, and the result was serious enough to cause real anxiety for his life.

Poor tragic Ahaziah! When we regard him from our modern viewpoint and judge him by what we know about the laws of psychology and heredity, we are inclined to look on him simply as the hopeless slave of fate, the helpless victim of bad ancestry and evil circumstance. We are inclined to expect his outlook to be embittered by the tragic misfortune that laid him so low. We are inclined to regard his downfall into evil practice and false worship as inevitable.

Yet the Bible insists that this man's downfall was not inevitable, and that he was not bound to follow in the footsteps of his father and mother. It insists that even Ahaziah was a potentially free man well able to choose which of the two very different paths in life he was going to walk on. He could choose what his career and destiny were to be.

In the background and environment of Ahaziah's life there were two widely different sources to which he could appeal for help in his hour of need. God, the living God, was there in the background of Ahaziah's life, and at any time in his career and especially during his tragic misfortune he could have looked to God for help. God was there, near at hand if he wanted Him, because Elijah was there near at hand if he wanted him. Ahaziah knew all about Elijah, and Carmel, and the lessons he had taught the nation. He had only to turn to Elijah in his illness and need and God was with him. God was there near at hand to be the counsellor and guide and friend to this young monarch because Elijah was there near at hand to be such a guide and helper. But the priests of Baal and the sanctuaries and altars of Baal were also there in the background of Ahaziah's life. Most of them had been cleared out of the land of Israel by the revolution under Elijah, but Ahaziah well knew exactly where he could send for help from the gods of his father and his mother if he cared to choose to look to Baal rather than to the Lord in his time of need.

Ahaziah then was free to choose. He certainly could not choose his parents, he could not choose the environment in which he was reared, but he could choose his God, for he was free to choose either the friendship and alliance of Elijah or the friendship and alliance of those who served Baal. Today we tend to make too much of the idea that whether a man is to be good or bad is determined not by his own choice but by his heredity and environment. It is true that no man can choose his father or mother and few can choose the environment in which they are to live their early life, yet every man can choose to what source he will turn in his hour of desperation and helplessness, and it is that choice which determines a man's destiny.

Henry Drummond has a story of a man who went to consult his doctor about his sight, and he was told that unless he gave up a certain way of life he would be blind in six months. Wistfully he turned to the window, looked out towards the sunshine streaming into the room and said, 'Farewell sweet light, for I cannot give up my sin'. That is the story not of a man who was helpless in the grip of evil, but of one who deliberately chose evil in the moment he was faced with the crisis of his existence. A Christian on the other hand is one who in the moment of his utter despair, when he has no power to choose his own way and to set himself free, nevertheless turns to Jesus Christ in his impotence, and seeks from Him the power to choose his freedom. Any man in this situation can choose Christ. And when Christ is there for him just as Elijah was there for Ahaziah, any man can choose his own freedom. Therefore you and I are judged by God not necessarily by the success we have made in controlling our lives, or by the measure of goodness we have attained, but by the direction in which we look for our help and strength. 'Look unto me, and be ye saved, all the ends of the earth.'[1] We can each one of us look, and because each one of us can look we are each free to choose.

Ahaziah Chooses and Finds Himself Judged

God stood in the background of Ahaziah's life, not prominently but unobtrusively. Elijah did not try to seize the occasion of the death of Ahab, Ahaziah's father, in order to bludgeon the mind of the young monarch with loud claims of the Lord for his loyalty. He did not force himself into prominence at

[1] Isa. 45.22

the court of Ahaziah during the first weeks of his reign. This was not because God did not care what happened. Of course He cared. Israel was His nation, Ahaziah was His child. All the time He was not indifferent but was watching over the affairs of Ahaziah and his realm, waiting and hoping for the turn towards Himself that would be a sign of Ahaziah's decision. Elijah was there all the time in the background ready to give advice or warning, approval or condemnation.

But Ahaziah, in the hour of his need, instead of looking to God and giving the sign of true faith for which God was waiting, chose to misinterpret God's unobtrusive gentleness in dealing with him. He decided to interpret it as meaning that God was either unreal or cared nothing and could be counted out. At the great crisis of his life, when he should have turned to the Lord in repentance, he declared by an act of public defiance that the one he believed in was Baal and not the Lord. To help himself through in his time of extremity he sent messengers to Baal-zebub the god of Ekron. This was a public sign to Israel that their king was a Baal worshipper. Ahaziah was now for the first time deliberately declaring that he had chosen to follow the ways of his father and mother rather than turn to the way pointed out by Elijah the prophet. It was a deliberate and calculated move.

Here is where we must be careful lest we repeat the tragic and yet deliberate mistake of Ahaziah. We are sometimes deluded about God. We think that because He does not seem to force Himself prominently forward into our own affairs, or into the affairs of the nation, or into international affairs, that He is not there at all. We think that because He is not there always giving clearly uttered warnings before we make our decisions that He is not so interested in us as are the tempting powers of evil which loudly clamour round us and force their claims upon us. Yet God *is* there to be sought by us, as Elijah was there to be sought by Ahaziah. He *is* there, in the background, partly hidden perhaps and yet keenly watching us. He is there in the person of Jesus Christ. He is waiting for us to decide to look to Him and He is easily to be found by us, if in the moment of our need we will turn to Him. 'Behold, I stand at the door, and knock,' said Jesus. 'If any man hear my voice, and open the door, I will come in to him, and will sup with him, and he with me.'[1] It is a tragedy when men refuse, even for a moment to listen for His knock and His voice, before they take the step of irrevocably rejecting His word and His help.

Ahaziah's action was a sign to Elijah that it was now time for him to interfere, and to confront Ahaziah with the Word of the Lord: '*But the angel of the Lord said to Elijah the Tishbite, Arise go up to meet the messengers of the king of Samaria, and say unto them, Is it not because there is not a God in Israel, that ye go to enquire of Baal-zebub the god of Ekron? Now therefore thus saith the Lord, Thou shalt not come down from that bed on which thou art gone up, but shalt surely die. And Elijah departed. And when the messengers turned back unto him, he said unto them, Why are ye now turned back? And they said unto him, There came a man to meet us, and said unto us, Go, turn again unto the king that sent you, and say unto him, Thus saith the Lord, Is it not because there is not a God in Israel, that thou sendest to enquire of Baal-zebub the god of Ekron? therefore thou shalt not come down from that bed on which thou art gone up, but shalt surely die. And he said unto them, What manner of man was he which came up to meet you, and told you these words? And they answered him, He was an hairy man, and girt with a girdle of leather about his loins. And he said, It is Elijah the Tishbite.*'

'*It is Elijah the Tishbite.*' It came as a shock to Ahaziah to realise that Elijah the Tishbite was one still to be reckoned with in Israel. It filled him with dismay to realise that Elijah had still such confidence in his cause as to interfere with the king's messengers in such an imperious way. He was filled with dismay and rage to discover that God was still there when he had hoped and indeed decided that God would not be there.

There follows now the grim part of this story which men find it difficult to believe and which preachers find it exceedingly difficult to talk about. In his anger Ahaziah determined to settle with Elijah. He had hitherto ignored him; now he was going to show his true attitude and fight him. He sent out fifty men to capture the prophet. Poor foolish monarch! His father had sent out army after army to capture Elijah during the years of famine and their attempt had failed. Ahaziah should have known that fifty men could not defeat God's prophet. He should have ceased troubling Elijah after

[1] Rev. 3.20

the terrible fate that overtook his first company of men. But again and yet again the expedition was repeated, with the result that the fear of Elijah and of Elijah's God brought the suppliant trembling captain to Elijah's feet to plead for mercy, and Elijah was able without any fear to walk into the presence of a hostile court and to confront Ahaziah in person with the word of judgment against which he had sought to vent his anger and spite.

Vicious King or Fiery Prophet?

What are we to say about the last part of this history of Ahaziah—the story of how Elijah called down fire from Heaven to consume the soldiers of Ahaziah? No one would suggest that this incident is recorded to show us how we should treat our enemies. When James and John wanted our Lord to follow the example of Elijah in this respect He rebuked them, saying, 'Ye know not what manner of spirit ye are of.'[1] Indeed we may take it that Elijah is here misunderstanding his mission and misrepresenting his Lord, just as Moses and David and other Old Testamant heroes did on occasion. One Old Testament critic says that this is 'the only painful episode in the whole history of Elijah', and he goes on to suggest that it fits so little into the true character of Elijah as portrayed elsewhere that the story is not true to life and was written about Elijah by one who did not understand him.

Such a theory certainly solves many moral problems and prevents any slur being cast on Elijah, but to accept it prevents us from taking from this story what is today a lesson many of us desperately need to learn. Elijah may have given a most unworthy representation of the true nature of God and yet God protected him and used him. In this conflict between the vicious and rebellious king and the foolish and unworthy prophet God took the side of the prophet. He did not withdraw His help from Elijah because Elijah made a callous and dramatic fool of himself. He did not wait until one side was prepared to behave in a perfectly holy manner before He chose which side He was to be on. God in the Old Testament reveals Himself as a God who takes sides in the terrible and bitter conflicts that must be fought in this world, where the

[1] Luke 9.55

only weapons are sometimes crude and brutal and destructive and where the lives of the purest servants of God often fail miserably. We must think more deeply into the meaning of the verse, 'If it had not been the Lord who was on our side, when men rose up against us: Then they had swallowed us up quick'.[1] And we must think more deeply into the meaning of the vision that Joshua had when, entering the land of Canaan with little force at his back, he saw the captain of the Lord of Hosts before him with a drawn sword in his hand—the Lord ready to take sides in that bitter conflict on which so much of the future of this world depended.

We who have felt called to serve God in the struggle against evil powers today are often as mistaken, self-centred and stupid as Elijah was in his behaviour on that mountain. We too sometimes descend to the same low level as Elijah on that day. And we wonder if God can use us at all. No Church is ever perfect. Yet through a miracle of grace in the midst of the compromised witness of the Church God is not ashamed to give His alliance to His people. He will even send His fire from Heaven to bear witness with us that we are on His side. There are those who are too good for the Church, but Christ was never too good for His Church in the days of His flesh, and is never too good for His Church today.

If in those far-off days God honoured His foolish, mistaken, ageing servant Elijah by sending fire from Heaven, there is hope for us that in spite of our misunderstanding of His purpose and our inadequacy truly to represent Him before men, He will nevertheless send down upon us His Spirit, and honour the ministry and the service which we are called to render in His name.

[1] Ps. 124.2-3

ELISHA SUCCEEDS TO HIS TASK

And it came to pass, when the Lord would take up Elijah into heaven by a whirlwind, that Elijah went with Elisha from Gilgal. And Elijah said unto Elisha, Tarry here, I pray thee; for the Lord hath sent me to Beth-el. And Elisha said unto him, As the Lord liveth, and as thy soul liveth, I will not leave thee. So they went down to Beth-el. And the sons of the prophets that were at Beth-el came forth to Elisha, and said unto him, Knowest thou that the Lord will take away thy master from thy head today? And he said, Yea, I know it; hold ye your peace. And Elijah said unto him, Elisha, tarry here, I pray thee; for the Lord hath sent me to Jericho. And he said, As the Lord liveth, and as thy soul liveth, I will not leave thee. So they came to Jericho. And the sons of the prophets that were at Jericho came to Elisha, and said unto him, Knowest thou that the Lord will take away thy master from thy head today? And he answered, Yea, I know it; hold ye your peace. And Elijah said unto him, Tarry, I pray thee, here; for the Lord hath sent me to Jordan. And he said, As the Lord liveth, and as thy soul liveth, I will not leave thee. And they two went on. And fifty men of the sons of the prophets went, and stood to view afar off: and they two stood by Jordan. And Elijah took his mantle, and wrapped it together, and smote the waters, and they were divided hither and thither, so that they two went over on dry ground. And it came to pass, when they were gone over, that Elijah said unto Elisha, Ask what I shall do for thee, before I be taken away from thee. And Elisha said, I pray thee, let a double portion of thy spirit be upon me. And he said, Thou hast asked a hard thing: nevertheless, if thou see me when I am taken from thee, it shall be so unto thee; but if not, it shall not be so. And it came to pass, as they still went on, and talked, that, behold, there appeared a chariot of fire, and horses of fire, and parted them both asunder; and Elijah went up by a whirlwind into heaven. And Elisha saw it, and he cried, My father, my father, the chariot of Israel, and the horsemen thereof. And he saw him no more: and he took hold of his own clothes, and rent them in two pieces. He took up also the mantle of Elijah that fell from him, and went back, and stood by the bank of Jordan; And he took the mantle of Elijah that fell from him, and smote the waters, and said, Where is the Lord God of Elijah? And when he also had smitten the waters, they parted hither and thither: and Elisha went over. And when the sons of the prophets which were to view at Jericho saw him, they said, The spirit of Elijah doth rest on Elisha. And they came to meet him, and bowed themselves to the ground before him.

2 KINGS 2.1-15

Let a Double Portion of thy Spirit be upon me!

'*And it came to pass, when the Lord would take up Elijah into heaven by a whirlwind, that Elijah went with Elisha from Gilgal.*'

Elijah had only a few more hours to live on this earth. His work was finished. For years he had been a feared and eminent figure in the life of his nation. He had given men a strong and firm lead in days of desperate crisis. At times the cause of God had seemed to depend on him alone in Israel.

And now God was going to take him from the life of Church and nation and there was to be left in his place an untried man, Elisha, who as yet had done nothing to prove whether or not he would be worthy. It is possible that many of the other prophets of the time were doubtful about Elisha's ability to take up the task of his great forerunner from whom he differed so greatly in character and in temperament. We can make this conjecture from the remarks they made as Elijah and Elisha passed through their sanctuaries.

In this chapter we see Elisha coming for the first time in his life hard up against responsibility in the task that was to be his in the cause of God. It was a second decisive day in his life. The first was ten years ago when Elijah first came to him and called him from following his plough to be his disciple and future successor. For ten years now he had been Elijah's servant and pupil. He had learned from him much about God, and life, and the task that needed to be done in Israel and the traditions he had to uphold.

As far as we can attempt from our modern standpoint to understand the feelings of these two men, at the beginning of this fateful day of parting it seems likely that Elijah felt he wanted to be rid of Elisha before the end came. Both men seemed to have sensed that the end was near, and the dying master announced to his young disciple that he was going to visit some of the schools of the prophets that he had established here and there in the neighbourhood. It was to be a short tour of farewell. He wanted to go alone. This would have been a perfectly natural wish. He had lived most of his life alone. He had faced all the crises of his life alone, and even though he felt called to pay a farewell visit to those he had worked with, he nevertheless in this final crisis felt drawn to the solitude of those mountain regions where Moses his great predecessor had also died unseen and in solitude. Alone and single-handed Elijah had fought his great battles for God. Alone and single-handed he wanted to fight death and to wait for the heavenly chariots to come for him. '*Tarry here, I pray thee,*' he said to Elisha, '*for the Lord hath sent me to Bethel.*'

But the young disciple clung to his master: '*As the Lord liveth, and as thy soul liveth, I will not leave thee.*' He clung thus because he could not bear to think of himself left alone to face his task for God in this world. Three times Elijah tried to get rid of Elisha. Three times the young man refused to leave his old father in God. Twice on their journey round the sanctuaries the local prophets came to Elisha to say to him, '*Knowest thou that the Lord will take away thy master from thy head today?*' Did he realise that he was to be left in charge and was he ready for the charge? But Elisha answered them with a short-tempered rebuke which reveals how much he was troubled: '*Yea, I know it; hold ye your peace.*' It is obvious that Elisha felt that there was yet something he needed if he was to face the task alone. He felt there was yet something that Elijah could help him to get before he went. Till then his only comfort and hope was to keep by Elijah.

They came to Jordan, Elijah still trying to get away by himself, Elisha still clinging to his company, and when Elijah saw that the younger man was still importunate enough and bold enough to follow him through the divided waters of Jordan, something seemed to make him relent. Perhaps, seeing Elisha's real anxiety, he felt he was not being fair to his pupil to cut him off from himself in such a state of mind even on his last day, if he could do anything more for him. '*Ask what I shall do for thee,*' he said, '*before I be taken away from thee.*' Like a flash Elisha had his final request formed in bold clear words: '*I pray thee, let a double portion of thy spirit be upon me.*'

Elisha saw clearly now that the old man before him had succeeded in his work as a prophet not because of his natural courage or power of speech or organising ability but simply because he had been given in abundant measure the gift of the Spirit of God. But though Elijah had done much for him during those past ten years of training he had not passed on to him the gift of the Spirit, nor had he told him how he could

F

receive the Spirit. Could Elijah even in his last hours on earth not do something to make up this great lack in his preparation for the task before him?

What Elisha in his desperate prayer confessed as lacking in his life indicates with only too much truth why our own attempts to live the Christian life often fail. We know how we ought to live, we have a clear understanding of the task we must undertake, we have been brought up in the best traditions and teaching of the Church, and yet we fail because we do not sufficiently experience the inward power of the living Spirit of God in our hearts. The Christian life is the result of an inward miracle. For if we are to live the Christian life Jesus Christ must be born within us and must be formed within us and grow within us through the work of the Holy Spirit in our hearts. It is in this way that we are enabled to become less self-centred and more disciplined and loving in our ways. But for this inward miracle we depend not on our own efforts, not on any method or technique, but on the work of God's Spirit.

Our religious education also sometimes fails in this respect. We can store the minds of those we teach with the knowledge of the Bible, with a Christian outlook that will help them to know how they should conduct themselves. We can train them in the technique required for various kinds of Church and Mission work. But we sometimes forget that all our teaching about God will go for nothing unless it is grasped as living truth by the power of the Spirit of God working in the minds of those we teach. And we forget that no matter how we teach men the way to live the Christian life and the technique of witnessing to others, that too will be in vain unless we at the same time make them aware that there is available the living power of the Spirit of God to enable them in all their efforts to serve God. Our religious education will fail unless we can also do something to help to bring those we teach into living fellowship with the Spirit of God who has been poured out upon the Church by Jesus Christ in order to enter men's hearts.

THOU HAST ASKED A HARD THING

It is impossible for one man to give himself or another the Spirit of God. '*Thou hast asked a hard thing*,' said Elijah. The Spirit of God is like the wind, Jesus once said, which 'bloweth where it listeth, and thou hearest the sound thereof, but canst not tell whence it cometh, and whither it goeth'.[1] If we can neither command nor manœuvre the wind so that it comes to blow upon our face, neither can we command or manœuvre the Spirit of God to come into our own life or the life of another. Ten years earlier Elijah had laid his mantle upon Elisha as a sign that he was to be his successor, but even a solemn ceremony such as that had not brought the Spirit of God upon Elisha. The Spirit of God is at the beck and call of no man, and is not tied to any ceremony we perform, however sacred. It is undoubtedly a '*hard thing*' men ask when they come to us in their need and plead with us to help them to receive the Spirit of God.

But Elijah could promise one thing with absolute confidence to his disciple. He knew without any doubt that God called Elisha ten years before to be his own successor in Israel. Therefore he felt certain that God would not fail to equip Elisha for the task to which He had called him. God might make him wait till the very last moment before He endowed Elisha with the gifts and the confidence he needed for the task. God does not always give His gifts to men before they are needed for use. He makes men wait in faith for a gift until the very moment that it is required. Could Elisha wait in faith and faithfulness to the very last moment? If he was found faithful at the end God would surely honour his faith. Elijah made a promise to Elisha that he would have the gift of the Spirit provided he remained faithful to the end: '*Thou hast asked a hard thing: nevertheless, if thou see me when I am taken from thee, it shall be so unto thee; but if not, it shall not be so.*'

There was perhaps another thought which crossed Elijah's mind in making this promise. He seemed to realise then that in those last hours he had to take Elisha into a greater intimacy with himself than he had ever before allowed him. He may have felt that he had been wrong in keeping himself detached and in reserve from this younger man now trembling before the approaching responsibility. After all they had been bound up in one task, in one bundle of life, in one office by God. Let Elisha stay beside him and watch him face whatever was coming, whether he saw him meet it with fear and trembling

[1] John 3.8

or with confidence and exultation. It might be that in that last hour together something might pass between them that would help to steady and strengthen his disciple for the uncertain future.

They went on and talked, says the story. In those last hours and in that last walk Elijah was perhaps opening his heart and mind to his servant as he had never done before.

There is one significant incident in the Gospel story that especially comes to our mind as we think about this last walk together of Elisha with Elijah, and remember the purpose that was in the hearts of these two men. As Jesus was facing His Cross two of the disciples, James and John, wanted to make sure that they would share in the powers and privileges of the glorious Kingdom they felt that Jesus was going to bring in. They came to Jesus and asked Him to grant that one of them might sit on His right hand and the other on His left hand when he entered His glory. In reply Jesus said, 'Can ye drink of the cup that I drink of? and be baptized with the baptism that I am baptized with?'[1] In that question He was asking them if they could share His sufferings and follow Him to His death on the Cross and remain, in fellowship with Him, faithful to the end. Then when James and John said they could follow Him in this way faithfully to His Cross and share His humiliation and death, Jesus challenged them to be content with doing this but to remember that to share in His power and glory was a gift that God alone could give to men. Then we see Jesus calling the disciples to follow Him on the way up to Jerusalem to the Cross and more and more talking with them and opening His heart to them. He had to lead them first to Calvary before they could be fit to receive the power of His Spirit that He was going to pour out upon men after He rose again. They had to experience Good Friday before they experienced the glory of Easter and Pentecost. They could not be rendered fit to carry on His work, or made great and strong by His Spirit for His service, till they had been involved in His humiliation and dying.

Such is still Jesus' answer to us today when we go to Him with the prayer to be given power and authority to do great things for Him by His Spirit. For to ask to be given the Spirit

[1] Mark 10.37-40

of Jesus Christ is to ask nothing less than a share in His Resurrection power and glory. When we ask Him this Jesus still says to us, 'Can ye drink of my cup?' We cannot share in the power of His Resurrection without in some way sharing in His death and humiliation. If we want to share in the power of the Spirit of Jesus Christ we must be willing to walk on with Him as He leads us to His Cross to watch His sufferings and as He seeks to draw us into more and more close intimacy with Himself. It is as men enter into deeper fellowship with Jesus Christ and especially with His sufferings that the power of His Spirit is imparted to them.

THE SPIRIT OF ELIJAH DOTH REST UPON ELISHA

We are not told how long Elijah and Elisha '*went on and talked*' before the final parting came. As they talked '*behold, there appeared a chariot of fire, and horses of fire, and parted them both asunder; and Elijah went up by a whirlwind into heaven. And Elisha saw it.*'

Elisha's first reaction was to tremble with utter dismay and grief. '*My father, my father,*' he cried, '*the chariot of Israel, and the horsemen thereof.*' He mourned as a son for the loss of a father. It was a personal bereavement as close and keen as any man can suffer. He mourned also as a leader of a nation for the loss of an army. It was a national calamity that had taken place. Not the most complete and devastating military defeat, involving the loss of all its horsemen and chariots, could be more terrible a calamity to Israel than the loss of this great man.

But then as he stood and turned his gaze from Heaven down to the earth he saw that the mantle of Elijah which fell from him as the chariot rose to Heaven was now there lying at his feet. He took heart and a new spirit immediately seemed to be given him, for he knew what that mantle at his feet meant. It was a renewal of God's call to him to take Elijah's place. It was a renewed sign of God's favour. With it was bound to go the fulfilment of the promise made by Elijah that he would be given the Spirit by whom Elijah had done great things in his day.

The immediate effect of the Spirit coming upon Elisha was that he found confidence in facing his task in the service of

God. Where before he trembled and shrank, now he was bold almost to the point of tempting God. He suddenly became bold enough to make a daring test of his power in the sight of fifty of the prophets who were standing afar off. '*He took up also the mantle of Elijah that fell from him, and went back and stood by the bank of Jordan; And he took the mantle of Elijah that fell from him, and smote the waters and said, Where is the Lord God of Elijah? and when he also had smitten the waters, they parted hither and thither: and Elisha went over. And when the sons of the prophets which were to view at Jericho saw him, they said, The spirit of Elijah doth rest on Elisha. And they came to meet him, and bowed themselves to the ground before him.*' The trembling Elisha had suddenly become their acknowledged leader and a bold man of action.

The Holy Spirit can give the same confidence and boldness today even to those who may be in themselves naturally timid and reserved. The early disciples before they received the Holy Spirit in power at Pentecost were afraid of the Jews and unable to face their task in the world. But after the Spirit was given them at Pentecost they witnessed and preached and faced men's threats with such lack of any sign of fear that men marvelled at their boldness. Many a man has shrunk from his task and felt, like Elisha, completely unable to face it but has received the needed gift of confidence when God's Spirit came into his heart. We can think of Moses, Gideon and Jeremiah who all shrank and trembled when God's call came to them and responsibility was laid on them. No one in his early life trembled more than Martin Luther at the thought of the impossibility of ever serving God worthily and effectively. And even the bold John Knox at St Andrews tried to evade the responsibility of ministering the Word of God by the plea that God had not called him, and after he had been forced against his will to accept the call to be preacher, he was for days troubled in mind as he thought of his task.

The boldness that is the gift of the Spirit is therefore something completely different from self-confidence. It is the boldness of the man who has trembled and trembles still because he has no confidence in himself. He has confidence because he trusts in God alone and not in himself. He is confident in God because the Spirit of sonship in his heart enables him to know that he is indeed a child of God—one who can cry boldly in prayer Abba Father, and who knows therefore that God's love will never forsake him nor God's power fail him.

Elisha's new-found confidence in God through the Spirit was partly due to the fact that he knew that the mantle of Elijah had fallen at his feet from Heaven and that he was able to pick it up and put it on himself. He had had that same mantle laid upon his shoulders by God through the hand of Elijah years before. It was only now that he recognised fully that it was indeed being offered to him as a sign given not by man but by Heaven itself. It was a sign of God's favour and a pledge that He would bestow on him the Spirit. God would never mock him by giving him in this way the outward sign that he was God's chosen servant without at the same time giving him inwardly the power of the Spirit he had so desperately and faithfully sought.

We do not have Elijah's mantle to be a sign to us of God's gift of His Spirit, but we nevertheless have the sign of our own Baptism. Like Elijah's mantle, Baptism helps us to receive the Holy Spirit and to know that we have received the Holy Spirit. Most of us are baptized when we are infants. It is God who then gives us this sign as a pledge of His call to us and as a pledge and promise of the gift of His Spirit. Many of us are apt to neglect the tremendous significance of the fact that we have been baptized. We are apt to think of it merely as a ceremony that the minister and our parents performed over us that can do nothing great or marvellous to us. But God means us to see in our Baptism what Elisha saw in that mantle of Elijah. He means us to see it as a pledge of the gift of His Spirit. He means us to see it as something done to us not by the hand of man but by His own hand from Heaven. And when we look on it in this way we realise that God will never mock us by giving us an outward sign of the pouring out of His Spirit upon us without giving us at the same time in reality and power the living Spirit in our hearts. God means us then to let our Baptism be to us a sign that can bring the Spirit more and more into our hearts by faith, and that can make us more and more confident in the knowledge that we have indeed received the Spirit of God.

How different Elijah and Elisha were. They were different

in temperament. Their tastes were different. Yet the same Spirit of God rested upon and inspired both. How different are we from these men of old. Our age, our circumstances, our ideals, the kind of life we are meant to live, are all different. And yet we live by the same Spirit, and we can rejoice in this wonderful fact today, that the '*spirit of Elijah doth rest on Elisha*'. In spite of our weakness and our inadequacy for the task of God in our generation, the same mighty Spirit which has fitted trembling men as weak as ourselves for great tasks, can fit us today. '*Where is the Lord God of Elijah?*' He worked through Elisha. He worked through trembling Jeremiah and Isaiah. He, the same Lord, can work today through anyone who will throw himself at His disposal in utter humility, realising, as Elisha did, that it is not by our natural capabilities that God works, but solely by His Spirit. The weak in our generation can be great for God if they will only tremble and cling to God and become as a little child before Him. When Moses had been taken from Israel and Joshua entered his task for God alone, the Lord said to him, 'As I was with Moses, so I will be with thee: I will not fail thee, nor forsake thee. Be strong and of a good courage.'[1] This is one of the deepest mysteries of the New Testament too—the mystery of 'Jesus Christ the same yesterday, and today, and forever'.[2]

[1] Josh. 1.5-6.   [2] Heb. 13.8

AT JERICHO AND BETHEL

And the men of the city said unto Elisha, Behold, I pray thee, the situation of this city is pleasant, as my lord seeth: but the water is naught, and the ground barren. And he said, Bring me a new cruse, and put salt therein. And they brought it to him. And he went forth unto the spring of the waters, and cast the salt in there, and said, Thus saith the Lord, I have healed these waters; there shall not be from thence any more death or barren land. So the waters were healed unto this day, according to the saying of Elisha which he spake. And he went up from thence unto Beth-el: and as he was going up by the way, there came forth little children out of the city, and mocked him, and said unto him, Go up, thou bald head; go up, thou bald head. And he turned back, and looked on them, and cursed them in the name of the Lord. And there came forth two she bears out of the wood, and tare forty and two children of them. And he went from thence to mount Carmel, and from thence he returned to Samaria.

2 KINGS 2.19-25

THE HUMAN SITUATION

Jericho was from all outward appearances a fine city. '*Behold*,' they said of it, '*the situation of this city is pleasant.*' It should have been an ideal place to live in for a great deal of money had been spent on it. No doubt the best architects and town planners of the day had had a hand in building it and the natural situation was ideal. But there was something wrong. The water in the wells, which was the vital source of the very life of this town, was poisoned by some hidden and very deep source of pollution, which no one could cure. The poison seemed to be the cause of a great deal of miscarriage both among the people and among the cattle and the sheep. Nothing was really healthy. Affairs became desperate in this well-organised and well-built city of Jericho. It looked as if the people would have to abandon the town. The more religious and serious inhabitants remembered that God had cursed the district in days of old when Joshua had sacked the city, and they felt that this curse of the Lord was now visiting its new inhabitants. The simpler people said that there was an evil spirit in the well.

But there was very little that they could do about it. They could neither trace the source of the poison nor think out any cure for the waters. They could plan and build a pleasant town on a pleasant site, but it was not within the scope of their ability to bring freshness and health into those bitter streams that were flowing through their aqueducts and pouring death into their towns. They went to Elisha and said, '*Behold, I pray thee, the situation of this city is pleasant, as my lord seeth, but the water is naught, and the ground barren.*'

We are constantly having to make plans for the reconstruction of human society today. We want to rebuild it on better lines than those of the past, to improve social and industrial conditions and the relationships between man and man. Our aim is to produce a more pleasant situation on earth for everybody—especially the poor and the weak. All this constant planning and reconstruction is good and necessary. But Jesus said, 'Out of the heart proceed evil thoughts, murders, adulteries, fornications, thefts, false witness, blasphemies: These are the things which defile a man.'[1] The tragedy constantly occurs that what should be an ideal and pleasant situation in human life, and a workable solution for the problems of society and industry, is often spoiled because in it we are dealing with human beings from whose hearts can flow a bitterness that can turn even a Paradise into a Hell, and a critical situation appears just when we had expected to see success crowning good and wise planning.

The Word that goes to the Heart of the Problem

How are we to sweeten the death-dealing waters? How are we to find a way of getting right down into the springs and motives of the hearts of men with transforming power, and of changing their inward outlook and attitude and ways of thinking? How are we to replace the lust for power and the love of money with the true motive of love for our fellowmen? How are we to replace the cynical spirit that believes that all human enterprise is motivated by purely materialistic consideration and selfish ends with that faith in God and faith in man that can alone be the basis for healthy and successful human enterprise?

[1] Matt. 15.19-20

It is significant that the men of Jericho turned to Elisha the prophet in their need. They felt that in turning to him they were turning to God. Elisha was no expert on water supply or town planning, but he was a man of God. The expert could only recommend ways of cleaning out the water channels and of building new aqueducts. Perhaps the man of God could do something more radical. Their turning to Elisha was a gesture which acknowledged their despair in human power and their faith that the cure must come from God alone.

Elisha '*went forth unto the spring of the waters*'. He went to the heart of the problem from the start, and throwing a cruse of salt into the very source of the poison, by the Word of God he cleansed the spring henceforth. '*Thus saith the Lord, I have healed these waters; there shall not be from thence any more death or barren land.*' It was by the Word of God that Elisha met the desperate need of Jericho.

Like the men of Jericho, the builders of society are looking to the Church for the help that they know they need in order to get to the heart and root of the real problem of human life. There is at least this sign of hope in the modern situation in many lands. Disillusionment over the failure of social planning has made some who never before acknowledged the need for God at least feel that the Church with the Gospel of Christ may perhaps have the power so to change the hearts of men that the bitter waters that frustrate the plans of even the wisest government may be sweetened, and become healthful and life-giving. The Church therefore stands in a position of great opportunity and great responsibility within the nations and between the nations.

But we must indeed go to the heart of the problem when disillusioned and frustrated men and women whose plans have failed wretchedly come round us because they have no clue to the meaning or the cure of life's deepest problems. If we are to be faithful in our duty to society itself, we must not talk merely in terms of new plans and new systems, but of the cure for the heart that Jesus Christ can give. For Jesus not only told men that the evils that mar society proceed from bitterness of the heart of man, He also offered a cure for the bitterness of the heart, and a promise that He could transform what springs from the heart of man. 'He that believeth on me,' He said, 'out of his belly shall flow rivers of living water.' (But this spake he of the Spirit, which they that believe on him should receive.)'[1]

It is by His Word that Jesus Christ goes to the heart of the problem. The cleansing and renewing Spirit of Jesus Christ is breathed into men's hearts as they listen to His Word. After Jesus rose again He breathed on His disciples and said to them, 'Receive ye the Holy Ghost.'[2] As He spoke He breathed into their hearts new life and a new Spirit. That is a sign of what Jesus is always ready to do for men today. He is always seeking to speak to them, to cause them to hear His voice. Whenever His Word is preached in the Church, and in various other ways, He speaks to men today with His loving voice. As He speaks He is seeking to breathe His Spirit into the hearts of those who will have faith, in the Word He speaks. His Word indeed can convey a new Spirit into the hearts of men, if men will listen to it and receive it deep into their minds and hearts and allow it to take root and work there. His Word can cleanse the spring of waters. 'Now ye are clean,' He once said to His disciples, 'through the word which I have spoken unto you.'[3]

The preaching of the Word of God in the midst of a nation's life is a more potent cure for the bitterness that spoils society than even those who preach it themselves sometimes realise. The motto of the city of Glasgow—'Let Glasgow flourish by the preaching of the Word'—was indeed coined by those who understood the social miracles that could be continually wrought when men opened their hearts to the Word proclaimed by the preacher in the pulpit, and to the living Word who is witnessed to in the Holy Scriptures. What took place in Jericho has been repeated time and again in human history. The human situation, with its desperate and apparently insoluble problems, have been saved by the Word of God.

THE WORD OF JUDGMENT

In contrast to the men of Jericho, who turned to the Word of God in their need, there was another town, in a worse state than Jericho, which, in spite of its need, rejected the Word of God.

[1] John 7.38-9   [2] John 20.22   [3] John 15.3

After Elisha left Jericho, '*he went up from thence unto Bethel: and as he was going up by the way, there came forth little children out of the city, and mocked him, and said unto him, Go up, thou bald head; go up, thou bald head.*'

Bethel was the place where Jacob had his vision of the heavenly ladder. It was therefore a town strong in its past associations with the true worship of the Lord. But the people of Bethel had by now reacted against all this. They had taught their children insulting songs about God's prophets and they had encouraged the young folk of the town to mock the men of God. Some commentators think that the word translated 'little children' in the Authorised Version should probably be translated 'lads'. If this is so it makes the story only a little less grim and repulsive to our feelings, and contrary to what we wish might have happened. It means that when the word went round of Elisha's approach to Bethel things were said or had been said by the older folks that emboldened the lads of the village to go out and express the general attitude of the place in their songs of ribald mockery. The phrase in their song '*Go up, thou bald head*' is perhaps a cynical reference to the story of the translation of Elijah to Heaven. It is quite likely that the men of Bethel still adhered to the religion of Baal, and were sworn enemies of the prophets of God.

In Bethel, then, they did not want the Word of the Lord, and the Word that might have brought blessing to Bethel, as to Jericho, was turned into a curse, and brought woe and destruction.

We hate the details of this story, of how the forty louts of Bethel were consumed by she-bears who came out of the wood according to the word of Elisha. This is a part of the Old Testament which has troubled the Christian conscience probably more than any other. We are revolted at the 'ideas of God' which men could form from such a story. But if we are meant to form any 'ideas of God' at all, we are certainly not meant to form them first of all from stories like this. We are meant to take our ideas of God from Jesus Christ. Nevertheless a story like this in the Scripture can serve to remind us that there is a grim though controlled element of judgment in the attitude of Jesus Christ to those who reject the Word of God. We hear Him expressing this in the woes He called down on the city of Capernaum. We catch a glimpse of it also in His cursing of the fig tree, in which with the utmost love and gentleness He reminded His nation that the Word of God could and might curse as well as bless.

In language that must always shock those who refuse to believe that there is a grim element of judgment in the Christian message, the New Testament teaches us that if we will not receive the gracious ministry of blessing by which God seeks to cleanse and renew our lives, then the love and mercy of God which is freely offered to us either to accept or reject, either to honour or insult, is turned into its opposite, and will bring judgment and damnation upon us instead of blessing. The same ministry of grace which brought life and gladness and freedom to Jericho when men received it gladly brought judgment to Bethel when men rejected and mocked it. Paul says of the effects of his preaching: 'To the one we are the savour of death unto death; and to the other the savour of life unto life.'[1] When Jesus sent out His disciples He said, 'He that receiveth you receiveth me.'[2] But woe to that city which will not receive His disciples. To receive Him in receiving the Word is to receive blessing, to reject Him in rejecting the Word is to involve ourselves inevitably in a judgment more terrible than that of Sodom.[3] In the ninth chapter of John's Gospel Jesus and the Evangelist both teach that the light which He has brought into the world can cure the blindness of those who will believe till they more and more see the true glory of God in Jesus. But the same light has exactly the opposite effect upon the Pharisees, who the more they look on it with prejudiced and unresponsive eyes are surely and gradually blinded till they are unable to see at all. 'For judgment,' said Jesus, 'I am come into this world, that they which see not might see; and that they which see might be made blind.'[4]

A strange fact is that Jericho was a city which God had, years before, visited with a curse. Bethel was a place which centuries before God had visited with blessing. Now under Elisha things are reversed. Jericho is blessed and Bethel is cursed. Let us never imagine, the story says to us, that the

---

[1] 2 Cor. 2.16
[2] Matt. 10.40
[3] Matt. 10.14-15
[4] John 9.39

grace of God ever clings automatically either to a place or to a race. Nor let us imagine that the curse of God can cling to any locality or can be transmitted automatically from one generation to another. What matters is the decision that men and women make about the Word of God that confronts them here and now.

THE SIGN

The Word of God which healed the waters at Jericho was accompanied by a sign. As Elisha healed the waters by the Word, he also cast into them a new cruse which he had ordered men to fill with salt. Some commentators think that there is much hidden meaning in the fact that Elisha did this as he healed the waters. Some dwell on the fact that salt is bitter, and that therefore the sign of the cruse being thrown into the bitter waters teaches us that bitterness in human life can be cured only by bitter means. And this leads them to speak about the bitterness of Christ's Cross which is the real and fundamental cure for human life from which the Word of God always derives its power to heal. Others dwell on the fact that the cruse was new. And this leads them to speak about Jesus Christ as bringing something quite new into the life of the world. Others feel that the new cruse of salt is one of the details of the Old Testament best left unexplained.

And yet if we think neither about the bitterness of the salt nor about the newness of the cruse, but simply of the apparent pure futility of Elisha's action in throwing the cruse into the spring (as if a little salt could cure such poison!) then we may be led to a true assessment of its real meaning. What an apparently useless action—to throw a mere handful of salt into a stream that was to irrigate a whole wide area and cleanse and refresh a whole town—and to expect such a spectacular result! Yet what a powerful Word accompanied this little sign! '*I have healed these waters; there shall not be from thence any more death or barren land.*' The insignificant sign cannot be separated from the powerful Word. Both are bound up together in God's way of working in one momentous event.

As we think about all this our thoughts turn to Jesus Christ. He spoke and speaks today a powerful Word. He seeks to work miracles today through His Word. He offers us forgiveness and new life within the Church through His Word. But as He works today in our midst with power through His Word, He also uses signs. He uses water and bread and wine and makes signs to us in Baptism and the Lord's Supper of what He is seeking to do for us and of how He is seeking to act upon us through His Word. We sometimes think the water, the bread, the wine are very much the same as the cruse of salt—futile and insignificant things. So they are, and yet Christ as He uses the water and gives us the bread and wine accompanies them with such a powerful Word of cleansing and promise that we no longer dare say these signs matter nothing and we can dispense with them! Because Christ has attached His powerful Word to the use of the water and the bread and the wine, and has made the use of the Word inseparable from these elements in Baptism and the Lord's Supper, we must not separate what God has joined together. We must use these signs continually in the Church, believing that as they are used along with the Word, Jesus Christ Himself is indeed acting in our midst to cleanse us and refresh us in ways that are most momentous in their significance, powerful beyond all our understanding, and of so great mystery that in using them we must adore Him in our midst.

IN THE HOME OF THE WIDOW

Now there cried a certain woman of the wives of the sons of the prophets unto Elisha, saying, Thy servant my husband is dead; and thou knowest that thy servant did fear the Lord: and the creditor is come to take unto him my two sons to be bondmen. And Elisha said unto her, What shall I do for thee? tell me, what hast thou in the house? And she said, Thine handmaid hath not any thing in the house, save a pot of oil. Then he said, Go, borrow thee vessels abroad of all thy neighbours, even empty vessels; borrow not a few. And when thou art come in, thou shalt shut the door upon thee and upon thy sons, and shalt pour out into all those vessels, and thou shalt set aside that which is full. So she went from him, and shut the door upon her and upon her sons, who brought the vessels to her; and she poured out. And it came to pass, when the vessels were full, that she said unto her son, Bring me yet a vessel. And he said unto her, There is not a vessel more. And the oil stayed. Then she came and told the man of God. And he said, Go, sell the oil, and pay thy debt, and live thou and thy children of the rest.

2 KINGS 4.1-7

Neither Elijah nor Elisha left us any definite teaching about God. Unlike Amos and Hosea who followed them they left no material which could be gathered into a book. And yet we can learn about God from the attitude and actions and character of a prophet as well as from his writings. Hosea, for instance, who spoke a great deal about the love and tenderness of God, was obviously a man of the most sensitive and tender nature, and what he said about God was very closely related to his own experience of suffering during his early life. Amos, who emphasised the righteousness of God so strongly, was an austere man whose first passion in life was for justice.

When we read these stories of Elijah and Elisha we undoubtedly form some impression of the attitude towards men of the God they represent. Sometimes, as we watch them, they give a wrong impression of God. No one in the Bible, except Jesus Christ, lived a fully consistent life. And yet in spite of their defects of character, both Elijah and Elisha give us a true impression of certain aspects of God's way of dealing with men, even though it is a confused and very faint impression. If Elijah with his dynamic and distant character and bearing represents the God who is above human life and who ever remains the Lord, Elisha in his attitude and bearing represents the God who is near at hand to all men and who makes Himself accessible to all men, especially to the poor and the oppressed. This is especially brought out in this particular passage.

WHAT SHALL I DO FOR THEE?

In this fourth chapter of the second Book of Kings we are shown how God in His mercy visits the homes of two of His people with willingness to bless and readiness to help.

It is a relief to read those beautiful stories here, for during the eight preceding chapters the Book of Kings has been concerned mainly with war and international politics. We have been told how God works with kings, prophets and nations, overthrowing armies, delivering cities and determining the course of history. He is shown as the mighty God with the broad sweeping purposes who ultimately decides the issues in international and national crises. It is a relief, then, to come to this chapter and be suddenly reminded that that is not all that God does. For here we are shown a God who visits homes as well as palaces, parliament houses and battlefields. Here we are shown a God who is God not only of the nation but also of the individual. Here we are shown that the God who gives the stars motion and overrules the destiny of the peoples is also the One who hears the cries of the widow and the fatherless, and whose love covers the finest detail of our individual life with infinite understanding. Here we are shown that God's saving power not only acts in the great movements of history, but extends also to arranging the practical details of everyday life which make up the worries and trials of seemingly insignificant people.

This is a thought in which the writers of the Bible were never weary of rejoicing. 'My help cometh from the Lord, which made heaven and earth,'[1] cried the psalmist. The word 'my' is to be emphasised. I may be a puny man with trivial worries and mundane needs, yet I can pray to Him who made Heaven and earth out of nothing, and His help comes to me!

[1] Ps. 121.2

'He telleth the number of the stars,' says another psalmist. 'He calleth them all by their names.'[1] But in the previous verse he has already said, 'He healeth the broken in heart, and bindeth up their wounds.' We see all this embodied in Jesus. The figure we see moving through the New Testament is the figure of One who is Lord. He can command the devils, the waves and the fevers. He has His Word for the rulers of His nation. Yet He has compassion on the poor and the weak and the obscure folk. In the midst of a great thronging mob about Him, He had the sensitiveness to discern the timid touch of a trembling woman who had come to Him with her hidden trouble. He spent much of His time in dealing with individuals, and talking to them about their individual problems. We see Him with all His divine power visting the homes of Jairus, of Martha and Mary, of Simon's wife's mother, with power to meet whatever situation was causing sorrow or anxiety to the hearts of those who invited Him.

In the person of Elisha the people of his time obviously felt that the help of God was accessible to them. This woman could waylay Elisha as he travelled about. It is characteristic of Elisha, much more than of his predecessor Elijah, that he was always accessible to the ordinary man of his time. Even though he was sometimes rude and difficult in his dealings with kings and princes, he was approachable by humble people. We see him moving in and out amongst them as if he wanted to be available if they wanted him. Therefore it was easy for this woman to contact him and put her case to him, and immediately she did so she found him ready to discuss with her what could be done. *'What shall I do for thee?'* he said. With such an opening she could frankly discuss with him the problem that was threatening her home with disaster.

Again we are reminded of how Jesus went on foot throughout all the villages of Samaria and Judea, and made Himself accessible not only to the great people of the land but to anyone who cared to come to Him with his problems. On His way He could be stopped and laid hold of by ordinary men and women, by the widows, outcasts and sinners. *'What shall I do for thee?'* is a phrase that He must frequently have used as they stopped Him, and as He listened with infinite patience.

[1] Ps. 147.4

He is equally accessible to us. Today we have Him near us, this man of God who can be laid hold of by us in our need and distress. When we open our Bibles and read about Him, He comes to manifest Himself. He comes to us through the Word that is preached when we gather in the Church, round the Bible, and at the Lord's Table. It is there indeed that we are most likely to meet Him, for He keeps His promise to be with us as we seek Him in such ways. Yet He is still the Christ who goes about amongst men, making Himself easily accessible, especially where there is human need.

To pray is simply to lay hold of this man Jesus and tell Him our need. Jesus told us that prayer was laying hold of God in our distress, as this woman laid hold of Elisha, and telling Him about it. He Himself likened prayer to a desperate woman waylaying a judge and pestering him about her need till he was weary.[1] To pray is to ask Christ's deliverance in the evils and trials with which our life is surrounded. It is to bring our troubles to Jesus Christ who can understand them and have communion with us through them, for with compassionate and understanding heart, and remembering His own life on earth amidst all the cares and problems of the home at Nazareth, He wants to say to us, *'What shall I do for thee?'*

It was a tale of social injustice that this woman poured out into the ear of the prophet of God. She was being cruelly oppressed through no fault of her own. She had been forced through sheer poverty to contract debt. She could not help doing so. She had been neither lazy nor extravagant, but evil circumstances had forced her to pledge the freedom of her children as security for a loan of money. We cannot blame her for this when the alternative was starvation. Moreover, she neither imagined that the time would come when she would find herself unable to pay nor thought that her creditors who had seemed so sympathetic towards her in her need could change so soon and become so cruel and ruthless as to put the law in action against her. But they had done so, and unless she could pay immediately her children would be sold as slaves.

How could the prophets of the Old Testament avoid having a social conscience and forbear from calling for social reform

[1] Luke 18.1-8

when they kept in touch with the life and sufferings of the people in their homes like this? It was this pastoral care for the people suffering under oppression, even more than his vision of God's righteousness, that made Amos cry out in temple and court against social injustice and against the creditors who could act with such cruelty. In the work of the Church today such real and sympathetic pastoral care of the people and such voicing of the needs of the ordinary man in the realm of politics are bound to go hand in hand. Such watchfulness and sympathy on the part of the Church will be always needed, for even in the most complete welfare state there will always be the poor and defenceless whom the law, however good, cannot quite protect, and there will always be men as merciless as these creditors were to this widow.

WHAT HAST THOU?

Elisha made her first of all confess her complete helplessness. '*What hast thou?*' he asked, and she answered, '*Thine handmaid hath not anything in the house, save a pot of oil.*' Her answer meant simply that she had nothing. For in her eyes the pot of oil was nothing. She was not seriously offering this pot of oil to meet the situation. It would have been such a futile contribution that she could never have offered it unless the prophet had asked for it.

And yet she had something. She had faith. Her sense of her own desperation, her acquaintance with her husband's work and her knowledge of the God of Israel, had made her look away from herself to God in faith that He could help her through His servant. She believed. And God used her faith for her own deliverance. '*Go, borrow thee vessels abroad of all thy neighbours, even empty vessels; borrow not a few. And when thou art come in, thou shalt shut the door upon thee and upon thy sons, and shalt pour out into all those vessels, and thou shalt set aside that which is full.*' Before any miracle took place she was tested as to how far she could act on faith. The more faith she had, the more vessels she borrowed, the bigger the miracle was to be.

We recognise here at once what the Gospels teach us, both about our need for faith, and about the power of faith. When our Lord worked miracles He sought around Him an atmosphere of faith. It is true that He was not dependent on the faith of those whom He helped, for He did miracles to help men and women who had no faith at all. But it is equally true that He loved most to work where there was a response of genuine faith. He could do no mighty work in His own home town of Nazareth, because of the people's unbelief. 'According to your faith be it unto you,'[1] was his Word when men came to Him for healing.

As a first step towards bringing us to faith God sometimes asks us *'What hast thou?'* and seeks to get us to reply, 'Thy servant hath not anything.' For to have faith is simply to look to God alone for the fulfilment of all our need, and we can be helped to do this if we realise that we have nothing else in ourselves or about ourselves by which even to start trying to meet our need. It is easier to look exclusively towards God in faith if we can recognise our own complete inability to help ourselves. Our faith therefore tends to be strongest at those times when we have nothing else to look to except to God. To have faith is to present ourselves to God like one of those empty vessels waiting to be filled as by a miracle.

But besides her faith there was her willingness to obey God, and to put at His disposal the one pot of oil. She had felt that this pot of oil was nothing and yet the prophet had asked for it and she gave it as all that she had. The situation in this home was saved by a sheer miracle. Nevertheless it was a miracle worked through the obedience of the widow to the Word of God, and in a situation where God asked her to put at His disposal everything that she could. This miracle reminds us in several of its details of the first miracle Jesus performed, at the wedding in Cana of Galilee. There at Cana when the wine failed the success of the day and the happiness of the young couple were threatened, and the help of Jesus was called for. But in saving the situation Jesus called for obedience. 'Whatsoever he saith unto you, do it,'[2] said Mary His mother to the servants. They had to fill the water pots with water and draw it out and serve it to the guests. God, when He works by miracle, can at the same time demand from us that we put everything we have at His disposal, in an act of obedience, even though we do not understand what is to be the final outcome.

[1] Matt. 9.29   [2] John 2.5

Go, Borrow . . . of all thy Neighbours

God used more than her own faith and obedience. He also used her neighbours. The situation was saved by the vessels she borrowed from those who lived round her. It is a pleasant relief to read of those neighbours, and to realise that in those days the world was peopled not only by creditors and thieves but also by ordinary people who were willing to act with kindness. We, too, in our own need, no matter how harshly this world has used us, must remember that sometimes God is seeking to help us through our neighbours, no less than He is seeking to help our neighbours through us. We can therefore thank Him that He gives us neighbours by whom He brings help and kindness and salvation into our lives. In the parable of the Good Samaritan the man who fell among thieves was a man whom life had treated brutally, but even he found a neighbour, whom God sent along in his time of need. The Apostle Paul found himself often helped through his neighbours. After his conversion he passed through a time of confusion and perplexity. But God did not come to him with help directly from Heaven in another spectacular vision. Instead, God blessed him through Ananias who became his neighbour.[1] In one of his letters we read a most significant verse: 'God . . . comforted us by the coming of Titus.'[2] God, when He wanted to refresh Paul, sent a neighbour through whom His influence, comfort and grace might be mediated to His Apostle. It is a tragedy to see Christians too proud or too nervous to seek or accept the help that can come to them in their need from fellow Christians. Often God means us to profit through the gifts He gives to our neighbour. Often, instead of sending us help directly from Heaven, He points us to our neighbour from whom we are meant to seek His help. Even Jesus was not too proud to refuse comfort and encouragement from friends and neighbours. He often went to the house of Martha and Mary, and of Lazarus, where His human heart was refreshed by friendship. He must have felt that such friendship at that time was a gift from His Heavenly Father. Let us not be too proud to be beholden to the neighbours who are God's gift to us.

In this part of the story we are reminded too that we are all

[1] Acts 9.10-17   [2] 2 Cor. 7.6

potential neighbours to others whom God is seeking to help. When the knock came to the door of those neighbours and this widow woman asked them to lend her their vessels, they were being offered the opportunity of sharing in God's compassionate and saving work even though they did not realise it. And how little they had to do! Their part was merely to lend a vessel, and perhaps an old cracked vessel at that.

Moreover, the whole miracle took place behind shut doors. *'When thou art come in, thou shalt shut the door upon thee and upon thy sons,'* said Elisha. She went from him and shut the door upon herself and upon her sons who brought the vessels to her. The neighbours did not see the wonderful use God made of the vessels they lent to this widow. They never realised just how gloriously God used the acts of kindness He challenged them to do to this poor woman. It is often so in life. As long as we live on this earth we may never know to what use God has put our cup of cold water, our cheerful greeting, our kind word, our helping hand, our little gift. In the great scene at the Judgment Throne in the parable of the sheep and the goats,[1] Jesus pictured Himself as saying to those who entered His glory, 'Come, ye blessed of my Father . . . for I was an hungred and ye gave me meat.' 'Lord, when saw we thee an hungred?' they said in surprise. The deeds God most uses to bring blessing to others may be the deeds we do almost unconsciously because we think they are insignificant. Indeed, they seem so small to us that we hardly know we are doing them. But behind the scenes, behind the shut doors, God is working through them His mighty miracles of grace and power.

If it is a great privilege to be used by God as neighbours in His works of compassion and grace in this world, it is, at the same time, a great responsibility to refuse to be used by God in this way. The parable of the sheep and the goats reminds us that when we meet a case of human need, Christ may be there personally challenging and testing us whether we are willing to be caught up into His redeeming purpose for men and women or whether we wish to be left forever out of that redeeming purpose. We are judged as to whether or not we accept the responsibility of playing the part of neighbour in the midst of God's saving activity in this world's life, and we

[1] Matt. 25.31-46

must remember that our neighbour is not just the man who lives next door. 'Who is my neighbour?'[1] said a lawyer once to Christ, and Jesus gave him a picture of a man lying in a desperate condition at the side of the way of life. Anyone, He taught, whom you meet in life's way who is in such need is your neighbour.

BORROW NOT A FEW

'So she went from him, and shut the door upon her and upon her sons, who brought the vessels to her; and she poured out. And it came to pass, when the vessels were full, that she said unto her son, Bring me yet a vessel. And he said unto her, There is not a vessel more. And the oil stayed.'

We continually limit God by our own unbelief, and our lack of expectancy. '*Borrow not a few*,' Elisha had said. God wanted to do more for this woman than He did. '*Bring me yet a vessel*,' she said to her son, but there was not a vessel more. How common a state of affairs this is in our own lives, and in the life of the Church. When we make preparations for God to act, they are never big enough. It is always lack of human vision that sets limitations to what God does in the Church, and that leaves us in spiritual poverty. And when we review what God has done with us in the past, we often realise we could have had much more from Him if we had been willing to expect more.

PAY THY DEBT AND LIVE

We are reminded here finally that when God pays our debts He does much more than pay our debts.

Then she came to the man of God and told him, and he said, '*Go, sell the oil, and pay thy debt, and live thou and thy children of the rest.*' He wiped out the debt at one blow, and gave her ample to live on, and we know that He would have given her more if her faith had been big enough to bring more vessels. Oil was a precious commodity. Oil meant wealth. God gave her oil to make her rich as well as free.

This is something we should all understand better than we do. It is true that Christ came to pay our debts. We had forfeited eternity, blessedness and freedom. The Cross means

[1] Luke 10.29

that we need no longer live in fear and bondage, under the powers of evil to which we had been sold. But when God paid our debts in Jesus Christ He at the same time wanted to make us infinitely rich. 'I am come that they might have life,' said Jesus, 'and that they might have it more abundantly.'[1] He did not come merely to pay our debts, bring us out of our prison and then leave us to fend for ourselves. God who 'spared not his own Son, but delivered him up for us all, how shall he not with him also freely give us all things?'[2] In the opening verses of the hundred and third Psalm we are reminded that God not only heals our diseases and forgives our iniquities but also crowns us with loving kindness and tender mercies, and satisfies us with abundance of good things. C. H. Spurgeon, commenting on this passage says something like this: 'When God lifts a man's head from the dust, he crowns him with a crown so heavy with His goodness that he could not wear it, were it not lined with the smooth velvet of His loving kindness.'

[1] John 10.10 [2] Rom. 8.32

THE SHUNAMMITE

And it fell on a day, that Elisha passed to Shunem, where was a great woman; and she constrained him to eat bread. And so it was, that as oft as he passed by, he turned in thither to eat bread. And she said unto her husband, Behold now, I perceive that this is an holy man of God, which passeth by us continually. Let us make a little chamber, I pray thee, on the wall; and let us set for him there a bed, and a table, and a stool, and a candlestick: and it shall be, when he cometh to us, that he shall turn in thither. And it fell on a day, that he came thither, and he turned into the chamber, and lay there. And he said to Gehazi his servant, Call this Shunammite. And when he had called her, she stood before him. And he said unto him, Say now unto her, Behold, thou hast been careful for us with all this care; what is to be done for thee? wouldest thou be spoken for to the king, or to the captain of the host? And she answered, I dwell among mine own people. And he said, What then is to be done for her? And Gehazi answered, Verily she hath no child, and her husband is old. And he said, Call her. And when he had called her, she stood in the door. And he said, About this season, according to the time of life, thou shalt embrace a son. And she said, Nay, my lord, thou man of God, do not lie unto thine handmaid. And the woman conceived, and bare a son at that season that Elisha had said unto her, according to the time of life. And when the child was grown, it fell on a day, that he went out to his father to the reapers. And he said unto his father, My head, my head. And he said to a lad, Carry him to his mother. And when he had taken him, and brought him to his mother, he sat on her knees till noon, and then died. And she went up, and laid him on the bed of the man of God, and shut the door upon him, and went out. And she called unto her husband, and said, Send me, I pray thee, one of the young men, and one of the asses, that I may run to the man of God, and come again. And he said, Wherefore wilt thou go to him today? it is neither new moon, nor sabbath. And she said, It shall be well. Then she saddled an ass, and said to her servant, Drive, and go forward; slack not thy riding for me, except I bid thee. So she went and came unto the man of God to mount Carmel. And it came to pass, when the man of God saw her afar off, that he said to Gehazi his servant, Behold, yonder is that Shunammite: Run now, I pray thee, to meet her, and say unto her, Is it well with thee? is it well with thy husband? is it well with the child? And she answered, It is well. And when she came to the man of God to the hill, she caught him by the feet: but Gehazi came near to thrust her away. And the man of God said, Let her alone; for her soul is vexed within her: and the Lord hath hid it from me, and hath not told me. Then she said, Did I desire a son of my lord? did I not say, Do not deceive me? Then he said to Gehazi, Gird up thy loins, and take my staff in thine hand, and go thy way: if thou meet any man, salute him not; and if any salute thee, answer him not again: and lay my staff upon the face of the child. And the mother of the child said, As the Lord liveth, and as thy soul liveth, I will not leave thee. And he arose, and followed her. And Gehazi passed on before them, and laid the staff upon the face of the child; but there was neither voice, nor hearing. Wherefore he went again to meet him, and told him, saying, The child is not awaked. And when Elisha was come into the house, behold, the child was dead, and laid upon his bed. He went in therefore, and shut the door upon them twain, and prayed unto the Lord. And he went up, and lay upon the child, and put his mouth upon his mouth, and his eyes upon his eyes, and his hands upon his hands: and he stretched himself upon the child, and the flesh of the child waxed warm. Then he returned, and walked in the house to and fro; and went up, and stretched himself upon him: and the child sneezed seven times, and the child opened his eyes. And he called Gehazi, and said, Call this Shunammite. So he called her. And when she was come in unto him, he said, Take up thy son. Then she went in, and fell at his feet, and bowed herself to the ground, and took up her son, and went out.

2 KINGS 4.8-37

A godly woman of Shunem put Elisha in her debt by her kindness to him. She had noticed him passing often to and fro by her house, and she made her home a haven of rest for him on his journeys. She put at Elisha's disposal a little chamber in her house which she and her husband had fitted up to suit his needs. Elisha offered to make some return for her services. He offered to use his influence with the king and the court to have some favour or advancement given to her or her family.

But the woman refused the offer with a quiet and dignified reply that bore witness to her contentment with her own lot and her sense of security in the surroundings in which God had put her. '*I dwell among mine own people,*' she said.

Gehazi, Elisha's servant, said to his master that one thing that could bring extra gladness into this woman's life was a child, and the word came to her: '*About this season, according to the time of life, thou shalt embrace a son.*' It is the fulfilment of this word that determines the rest of this story, for here we are taught vivid and important lessons about our attitude to the Word of God, and the possibility of its fulfilment in our own lives.

THE STAGGERING WORD OF GOD

This woman was old. She had ceased giving thought to such a possibility as this Word of God held out to her. In fact, when the Word of God came to her that day, she felt that these two men were mocking her. In her reply she tried to check her annoyance and anger at them for reviving her old disappointments, and reminding her of her reproach, for in the East childlessness was regarded as a stigma that signified reproach from God. But at the same time she found that she could not put the word out of her mind, for after all Elisha was the prophet of God. He had cleansed the waters of Jericho. He had done other mighty things through his word. And now his word had come to her clearly promising her without any possible ambiguity a miracle beyond her wildest dreams! She laughed, as Sarah had laughed at the word that came to her in her time. 'Nay,' she said, 'do not deceive me.' But in spite of her laughter she knew she must treasure up in her heart what had been promised in the name of God.

The Word of God which comes to us today appears also to hold out the same wild promises, which seem so impossible of fulfilment that we are tempted not to take them seriously and to put them out of our minds. The Word of God promises us that in spite of our fixed habits of mind and heart, our habitually distorted prejudices and ways can through the power of the Spirit of God be subdued and changed. The Word of God promises that in spite of what we are and have been all our days from our birth, we can become new creatures. The Word tells us that the past can be blotted out and a new start made in the sight of God through the blood of Jesus Christ which cleanses us from all sin. The Word tells us no less clearly and decisively than it told the woman of Shunem of a new birth from above that can make everything different and remove all our reproach in a completely staggering miracle of grace and power. The Word tells us that after death we shall be like Christ, for we shall see Him as He is, and our bodies which at present bear all the marks of corruption and humiliation will be recreated to become like the glorious body which Jesus had after His Resurrection. Moreover, it is a Word whose grace extends not only to ourselves but also to the children whom God gives to us.

When we hear the Word that comes to us through the Holy Scripture promising us all these things, we are tempted to say what the Shunammite woman said: 'Nay, do not deceive me.' We are tempted to say that the Word does not really mean quite what it seems to say. In order to make it less of a strain on our faith we believe the Word of God about ourselves and our possibilities in Christ, we interpret the Bible in such a way as to minimise the staggering greatness of what Christ holds out to us in His promises. Our Lord Himself understood that it would be difficult for us to believe when we listened to His Word. When He spoke some of His greatest promises about the life to come and saw the baffled and amazed look on His disciples' faces, He said, 'If it were not so, I would have told you.'[1] He means us to give all His words their utmost weight for He would never deceive us by using exaggerated terms.

A Challenge to Faith

The staggering Word of God was fulfilled: '*And the woman conceived and bare a son in that season that Elisha had said unto her.*' How wonderful it all seemed at first! The Word of God seemed to come easily to fruition. The woman bowed her head and believed it had happened. 'Believe that ye receive . . . , and ye shall have.'[2] All this can happen in our own experience of the Word of God, for to have it fulfilled in our life means the mere acceptance of what it offers us in all the simplicity of faith. We only need believe and accept God's Word, and what is promised is ours. Blessed are those who have discovered that in the mere acceptance of Christ and His promises without hard effort or hard work, there is here and now new life and hope.

How wonderful then, it seemed, was God's blessing on this home at Shunem during the early years of the life of this child! The child was a token to them that God was love, and God's Word was true. He was a token to them that the faith which accepts God's Word in pure undoubting simplicity will

[1] John 14.2   [2] Mark 11.24

never be ashamed. This woman could witness to others through this child while he ran in and out of her door. She could tell the story of how God gave him to her by a sheer miracle and by the word of the prophet. There are times for us ourselves, especially at the beginning of the Christian life, when to live by faith is like that. God's promises seem all to be fulfilled to us with almost automatic certainty. We have no cause to give way to gloomy doubts. We are surrounded by signs, even by manifest miracles, by which we can prove to our neighbours and friends that God's Word is true, and that those who trust Him shall have the desires of their hearts.

But after the passing of years there came a day when the woman of Shunem had to battle for the fulfilment of the very Word she had thought was fixed and firm. *'And when the child was grown, it fell on a day, that he went out to his father to the reapers. And he said unto his father, My head, my head. And he said to a lad, carry him to his mother. And when he had taken him, and brought him to his mother, he sat on her knees till noon, and then died. And she went up, and laid him on the bed of the man of God, and shut the door upon him, and went out.* The child was not very old, for she could pick him up and lay him on the prophet's bed.

He was dead. There are those who would say that in such a situation, if we believe in God, we will automatically believe that all this is exactly planned by God Himself, and we should therefore say: 'The Lord gave, and the Lord hath taken away; blessed be the name of the Lord.'[1] For after all—so the argument goes—death is death, and it is the Lord's will that we should accept death. But the faith that had been raised within this woman's heart by the Word of God made her take up a different attitude. She rebelled at what had happened. She said to herself that this could not be God's will. Indeed it must be the Devil's will. God had promised her a child, and He had not meant to mock her through that promise. She refused to allow herself even to imagine for a moment that God's will could fail in fulfilment. She refused to believe that this could be the end of the blessing that God had brought into her life when He gave her this child. After all, she had not even asked God for this child. He had come to her as a gift

[1] Job 1.21

spontaneously offered by Him out of His goodness. The Lord who had been responsible for bringing this sunshine into her life would make Himself responsible for seeing that it was kept there. She would refuse to accept the child's death as a final word.

Therefore she acted throughout as if this death was a short and accidental interlude in a story in which everything must turn out well. '*It shall be well,*' she said to her servants. She refused to say much more to anyone. To discuss it with others who did not understand what faith meant might have discouraged her. They might have spoken of accepting the situation. They might have spoken of funeral arrangements. '*It shall be well,*' she said to everyone, and she called for her ass and her servant and made for the prophet of God. Even with Gehazi, who was sent by Elisha to meet her, she refused to discuss the matter. All the time she wore a brave face. She refused even in her appearance to admit that the Word of God could possibly disappoint her. She did not relax or rest until she had got hold of Elisha the prophet, and then she poured out her wild and desperate feelings. She told him the whole story. She let him know that this matter was his responsibility, and she did not intend to let go of him until it was put right. '*Did I desire a son of my lord?*' she cried. '*Did I not say, Do not deceive me?*'

It was a strong argument. 'You,' she said to God's representative, 'you and your God interfered with my life in order to please me. I never asked nor sought this blessing. You forced it upon me, and I accepted it in good faith. I let my heart grow round this little one, for you encouraged me to expect that I had a right to the happiness he brought. It was a freely given reward for what I did in God's name. Now that it has been taken from me, I look to you to accept your responsibility to restore it. '*As the Lord liveth, and as thy soul liveth, I will not leave thee.*'

Such was the kind of faith that allowed God to fulfil His Word perfectly to this woman of Shunem. It was a faith that sought to lay hold and to keep hold, not only of the promises, but of the promiser. It was a faith that endured in the face of delay, and battled for the fulfilment of the Word against all contradiction. It was a faith that refused to accept from God only half a blessing but insisted on the full blessing. If this woman had accepted only the half blessing, and had buried her child, she would after all have received some benefit from the Word of God. Her reproach would have been removed. She would have had a few years of happiness to look back upon and some blessed memories to cheer her. She could have spoken to others of how God had once in a miraculous way answered her prayers and fulfilled her desires. After all, to receive all that from the Word of God would have been much better than to receive nothing from the Word of God! But she refused to allow God to stop halfway, and insisted on His going the whole way He had promised.

At certain times our faith is tried, as this woman's faith was tried, and we have to decide whether we are going to insist before God that He shall fulfil all His promises to us, or whether we are going to let Him stop halfway. In living our Christian lives we sometimes far too easily allow God to stop halfway in His blessing of us. We far too easily allow hopes and happinesses to die that should be living and increasing as the years pass. There is a place in our Christian life for refusing to accept what seems on the surface to be the will of God. There is a place for rebellion against circumstances that do not seem to be in line with what God has promised us of His grace and power in Christ.

When we read the New Testament, for instance, we are promised a large measure of victory in our struggle with evil in our own lives. We are told that God is able to 'keep you from falling'[1] and to do for us 'exceeding abundantly above all that we ask or think'.[2] We are promised that 'sin shall not have dominion'[3] over us. Such passages as we read them give us a new and great vision of the possible heights to which we can rise in our attempt to live the Christian life. It is God's Word that gives us this vision. We do not conjure it up by our own wishful thinking. Therefore, if we seem to be defeated and frustrated in its fulfilment, we must refuse to accept defeat as the last word. If God has promised us victory over the power of our besetting sin, we must not leave Him alone till He gives us victory. Faith, then, sometimes means rebelling against what seems to be God's will, in order that we may have God's

[1] Jude 24   [2] Eph. 3.20   [3] Rom. 6.14

will. It is rebellion against all circumstances that seem to us to belie God's promises.

When Jesus was near Tyre and Sidon a Syrophenician woman[1] came to Him and cried out, 'Have mercy on me, O Lord, thou Son of David; my daughter is grievously vexed with a devil.' Jesus at first answered her not a word. But the woman refused to take His silence as an indication of the attitude of His heart towards her, and she persisted in her request. The disciples tried to bully her away, but she still persisted. And then Jesus said to her, 'I am not sent but unto the lost sheep of the house of Israel.' It was as if He said, 'I didn't come to help such as you; go away!' But again the woman refused to believe that this rebuke revealed His true attitude. She persisted in spite of His rebuff, and she caught hold of Him: 'Lord help me.' Then Jesus added something else to put her off. 'It is not meet to take the children's bread, and to cast it to dogs,' He said. But the woman again refused to be put off. She believed that there must be love in His heart towards her in spite of appearances. She argued with Him and persisted in her request, and then Christ broke down all barriers and said, 'O woman, great is thy faith,' and her daughter was made whole.

Great is thy faith! Her faith was great, because she refused to accept appearances. She rebelled against circumstances that seemed to belie His power and love, and persisted. Faith will deal with God as the Syrophenician woman dealt with Jesus.

Of course there are times when we have to learn to resign ourselves. The Word of God does not promise to us today such spectacular and immediate physical miracles as it did to men and women who lived in the days of the apostles and prophets. We all know this only too well when death visits our homes and family circles, for then we have to resign ourselves like Job and say, 'The Lord gave, and the Lord hath taken away,'[2] But even in thus resigning ourselves in the days of mourning, we must refuse to entertain any thought that the death of our dear ones can be God's final Word to us about them. It is Jesus Christ who has made our earthy friendship infinitely precious to us. It is Jesus Christ who has made our Christian home life rich and pure to us. If Christ has blessed our

---

[1] Mark 7.24-30, Matt. 15.21-28   [2] Job 1.21

relationship with others, and has raised in our hearts such true hope that the ties we have with them are stronger than death itself, He will never disappoint the hopes He has raised in our hearts. Therefore we can commit our loved ones to Him with confidence, in the sure knowledge that, whether they live or die, all is well, for death can be only another interlude in a relationship and story that strain towards greater things in the world that is to come.

A CHALLENGE TO LOVE

Elisha saw the force of the woman's arguments, and sent on Gehazi carrying his staff, with detailed instructions how to perform the miracle. Gehazi had to perform such and such a ceremony over the child with the staff. He had to repeat certain words and see what happened. Gehazi passed on and fulfilled Elisha's instructions, but *there was neither voice, nor hearing*. It was not until Elisha personally devoted himself wholeheartedly to the task that any success was obtained. Even then, so difficult was the task that it required not a piece of ritualistic ceremony but a prolonged agony of prayer, inspired by personal concern both for the people he was dealing with and for the glory of the God he served.

This is all described in a vivid and detailed way. '*And he went up, and lay upon the child, and put his mouth upon his mouth, and his eyes upon his eyes, and his hands upon his hands: and he stretched himself upon the child; and the flesh of the child waxed warm. Then he returned, and walked in the house to and fro; and went up, and stretched himself upon him: and the child sneezed seven times, and the child opened his eyes.*'

What does this strange description of the child's resurrection tell us? It tells us that Elisha's work was blessed and crowned with success only when he sacrificed himself over the child, and sought, certainly in a crude and symbolic way, to enter into the very suffering and death of those to whom he was ministering. Before Elisha could be the minister of the power and love of God to this house, and be of real help to them in their distress, he had to give up all his dignity and act as if he were the distracted and suffering parent of the child. It was only then that he raised the child.

In our service of Christ today we are called to a task that

demands from us no less a miracle than that to which Elisha was called in the house at Shunem. When we face the world we are confronted with a great dead mass of indifference to the Gospel which it seems impossible to change. And when we look at ourselves in the Church we are forced to confess much spiritual deadness. Indeed even the Church has the appearance of the valley of dead bones (very many there were and they were very dry!) which was shown to Ezekiel[1] when God wanted to impress him with the true state of the Church in his day. 'Can these bones live?' is as real a question to us as to Ezekiel. Our task then in bringing the Word of God to the Church and to the world is to bring life where there is death, it is to bring glorious hope where there is now little else but despair. But we can never hope to fulfil that task without ourselves seeking to enter with real sacrifice and sympathy into the sorrows and conditions of those whom we are commissioned to serve in the name of Christ, and without allowing our hearts to enter into their lostness and despair and death.

Many suggestions are being made today as to how the Church can become more effective in its power to attract and hold men and women, to serve them in the name of Christ, and to manifest more real and living power within its own life. There are those who say that if we are to attract and hold men today, we need to appeal to them through more colourful and dramatic services. We need to develop a more elaborate and stately ritual. Others say that if we are to attract men we must have more informal Church services with more catchy musical accompaniment. Certainly we must constantly discuss all this and ask ourselves what is the best ritual to use in our services. But we must remember that all this is no more than a discussion of the best way of laying the staff upon the face of the dead child. No amount of ritual, whether it be high and stately and elaborate, or low and popular and informal, with even the best and most suitable musical accompaniment, will ever suffice to raise dead souls to life. Moreover, it is not enough for the preacher merely to say the correct things from the pulpit and expect that such preaching by itself will work miracles. It is true that we must have the correct doctrine. The Church must try to regain forgotten evangelical

---

[1] Ezek. 37

truths in its proclamation to the people. But let us realise that even correct language, and even Biblical language, may be no more effective than Gehazi's language was when he laid the staff on the face of the child and called it to life, and yet *'there was neither voice, nor hearing'*.

Perhaps the Church is weak and unimpressive in its effect today because we are not concerned enough to think and feel ourselves realistically into the situation of those who are living without faith in Jesus Christ. There is within our hearts little of that 'travail for souls', and that real agonising concern over the state of man outside of Christ that has been the concern of all the world's greatest evangelists—and the secret of their success. 'As soon as Zion travailed, she brought forth her children,'[1] said Isaiah, which is only another way of saying that in the work of God there must be travail on the part of some before there will be redemption of many. Perhaps we have to learn that the Church of Christ is built by our tears as well as by our work. Paul revealed the secret of his power as a church-builder when he gathered the elders of Ephesus together and reminded them of how for the space of three years, 'I ceased not to warn every one night and day with tears'.[2]

There are writers who see in this story a foreshadowing of the sacrifice of Jesus Christ. The story tells how the prophet, after other attempts had failed, humbled himself over the body of the dead boy and tried to make himself the same size. Here the imagination turns to Christ, who after everything else had failed, and the mere ritual of the Old Testament had proved impotent, was born a babe in the manger and made of like stature to His brethren. The story tells how Elisha breathed, as it were, his own life into the body of the child, and absorbed in its place in his own body the cold death that held the child. And here again the imagination turns in gratitude to Christ who bore our sins in His own body on the tree, and who, when He rose again from the dead, came and breathed upon the disciples His own life in the upper room, saying, 'Receive ye the Holy Ghost.'[3] Our Lord Jesus Christ, says Paul, 'though he was rich, yet for your sakes he became poor, that ye through his poverty might be rich'.[4]

[1] Isa. 66.8   [2] Acts 20.31   [3] John 20.22   [4] 2 Cor. 8.9

THREE MIRACLES

And Elisha came again to Gilgal: and there was a dearth in the land; and the sons of the prophets were sitting before him: and he said unto his servant, Set on the great pot, and seethe pottage for the sons of the prophets. And one went out into the field to gather herbs, and found a wild vine, and gathered thereof wild gourds his lap full, and came and shred them into the pot of pottage: for they knew them not. So they poured out for the men to eat. And it came to pass, as they were eaitng of the pottage, that they cried out, and said, O thou man of God, there is death in the pot. And they could not eat thereof. But he said, Then bring meal. And he cast it into the pot; and he said, Pour out for thy people, that they may eat. And there was no harm in the pot.

And there came a man from Baal-shalisha, and brought the man of God bread of the firstfruits, twenty loaves of barley, and full ears of corn in the husk thereof. And he said, Give unto the people, that they may eat. And his servitor said, What, should I set this before an hundred men? He said again, Give the people, that they may eat: for thus saith the Lord, They shall eat, and shall leave thereof. So he set it before them, and they did eat, and left thereof, according to the word of the Lord.

And the sons of the prophets said unto Elisha, Behold now, the place where we dwell with thee is too strait for us. Let us go, we pray thee, unto Jordan, and take thence every man a beam, and let us make us a place there, where we may dwell. And he answered, Go ye. And one said, Be content, I pray thee, and go with thy servants. And he answered, I will go. So he went with them. And when they came to Jordan, they cut down wood. But as one was felling a beam, the axe head fell into the water: and he cried, and said, Alas, master! for it was borrowed. And the man of God said, Where fell it? And he shewed him the place. And he cut down a stick, and cast it in thither; and the iron did swim. Therefore said he, Take it up to thee. And he put out his hand, and took it.

2 KINGS 4.38-44, 6.1-7

There is a readiness among many people who read the New Testament today to accept as historical the miracles recorded in it, as long as they can see some point in their being performed. Many people find little difficulty in believing that Jesus healed the sick, cast out evil spirits and stilled the storm.

They can believe even that Jesus raised the dead, for there was some point in His doing all that. When Jesus did these things, God's supernatural power worked through Him for great ends. These miracles demonstrate that the Kingdom of God has come. They show us that Jesus is the Messiah, and that His heart was moved with compassion for the sufferings of His fellow men.

But many people in reading the Bible feel that these miracle stories about Elisha's making an axe-head float or curing poisoned porridge are too like the things done by performing magicians and conjurors at carnivals to be credible. They find it hard to believe that the supernatural power of God—the same power which raised up Christ—could be at the disposal of Elisha for the trivial purposes which these miracles seem to serve at first sight to serve. Some writers who insist on the truth of the miraculous element in many parts of the Old Testament history are uncertain when they come to these stories of Elisha and confess feeling that here the sacred Scripture degenerates to the level of the stories of the mediæval saints and pagan magicians. All this is because they do not see any point in these stories.

But each of these three miracles has real purpose. Each is a typical example of how God's wonderful and gracious power can cover all the defects of our work for Him in the Church; for each of these three miracles was performed within the sphere of Church life. They were performed for the sake of three good men whose lives were dedicated to the service of God. Each story is the story of something that happened in the various 'schools of prophets', religious communities where men gathered to live and work together in the service of the Lord. We can regard these prophets as the Church workers of their day.

The man concerned in each of these miracle stories has tried to do his best in the service of his fellow prophets and of God. But, in spite of his wholehearted zeal and good intentions, something went wrong. Something was lacking. His zeal was misdirected. His work became spoiled. It was to meet such need in each case that Elisha worked a miracle.

Today it is those who respond with all that they have to the claims of Jesus Christ who begin to experience how wonderfully and powerfully God can work in ordinary daily life. 'Launch out into the deep,' said Jesus, 'and let down your nets for a draught.'[1] He was going to work a miracle of extraordinary grace and power, but first He told His disciples to commit themselves to obey His guidance and His command in a way that required complete faith in His word. They had to leave the shore in obedience to Him, then they beheld the glory revealed in His miraculous work. Perhaps if we were less critical of the Bible for its stories and miracles, and more willing to work for God wholeheartedly in fellowship with others, then we too would begin to see the miraculous happen in our own work.

Certainly these miracle stories come down to the level of mundane and apparently trivial things. They tell of miracles accomplished in the cookhouse and storehouse. But when we study the Gospels we find that our Lord Himself was not ashamed to do for His disciples things very similar. It may be, then, that He is prepared to do like things for ourselves in our present-day situations and difficulties, which are in so many ways, both in their triviality and in their pressing urgency, the same situations and the same difficulties as the people of God have faced in every age. It is this fact that forces us, in thinking of the possible significance of these three miracle stories for us now, to expound them as typical of what Jesus Christ would do within His Church today.

CHRIST AND OUR MISTAKES

'And Elisha came again to Gilgal: and there was a dearth in the land; and the sons of the prophets were sitting before him: and he said unto his servant, Set on the great pot, and seethe pottage for the sons of the prophets. And one went out into the fields to gather herbs, and found a wild vine, and gathered thereof wild gourds his lap full, and came and shred them into the pot of pottage: for they knew them not. So they poured out for the men to eat. And it came to pass, as they were eating of the pottage, that they cried out, and said, O thou man of God, there is death in the pot. And they could not eat thereof.'

A zealous worker in the service of God found a job in the cookhouse of one of the communities where the prophets lived together. His task was undoubtedly important at that

[1] Luke 5.4

particular time because the land was in the grip of a famine and food was scarce. Our man, full of zeal for God, determined to show it through his work in the kitchen. He was sent to collect herbs for the main meal of the day. This was cooked in one great pot, for those were the days of simple life. But he was a stranger to those parts around Gilgal. Perhaps he came from the north country where wild melons flourished and were much used for cooking. In his search for herbs he saw a plant that looked like wild melon. This plant, according to some commentators, is called colocynth. It grows abundantly by the Dead Sea and produces a fine-looking fruit, but it is, nevertheless, deadly poison. The man made the natural mistake. He thought that these poisonous fruits were wild melons. He gathered them and shredded them into the pot. In the middle of the meal the cry of alarm and despair was raised on all sides. Poison! Death! The precious rations were not only spoiled but there was the danger that those who had partaken might come to harm. It was a tragic mistake which might have had far-reaching effects, caused by the enthusiasm of the man who had committed it. Death in the pot!

As Elisha, by the power of God, was able to purge out the poison from the pottage which this zealous servant had made and cover over his mistakes, so Christ's miraculous power can cover over the mistakes we all make in His service. We can think of how Jesus, on three occasions, corrected the mistaken zeal of His followers in a most kindly way. Once James and John came to Him about the Samaritan village which had refused to receive the disciples of Jesus. They wanted it annihilated. 'Lord,' they cried, 'wilt thou that we command fire to come down from heaven, and consume them, even as Elias did?' Jesus turned and rebuked them, saying, 'Ye know not what manner of spirit ye are of.'[1] On another occasion, the temple tax-gatherers asked Peter if His Master paid the temple tax. Peter said, 'Certainly, He will pay it.' It was a mistake. Jesus was the Lord of the temple, and certainly did not need to pay any temple tax. He rebuked Peter again gently for his mistake, but he saved the awkward situation by making a fish come from the depth of the sea with a coin in

[1] Luke 9.54-55

its mouth, so that the tax was paid in a manner that in no way obscured His Lordship.[1] Thus Peter was rebuked, and yet his mistake was covered over. On another occasion the soldiers were coming to take Jesus by force, and one of His disciples, probably Peter, drew a sword, saying, 'Lord, shall we smite with the sword? And one of them smote the servant of the high priest, and cut off his right ear. And Jesus answered and said, Suffer ye thus far. And he touched his ear, and healed him.'[2]

Few of us do not need the assurance which such stories can bring us when we think over the follies we have committed sometimes through our attempts to serve Jesus Christ. For many of us the enthusiasm of our early days of Christian service was often marred by misdirected zeal and by a way of approaching other people more likely to do harm than good in the service of Jesus Christ. Few who have entered the ministry of the Gospel can remember the first few years of their ministry without realising that there was perhaps a certain amount of poison in what they gave their people. They did not know any better at the time. It can be an infinitely serious matter to make mistakes in the ministry of the Gospel, in teaching a Sunday School class, or in the discipline and management of the Churches, or in bringing up our own children. For in all this activity we are taking the responsibility of caring for souls for whom Jesus Christ has died. And yet mistakes are made! Mistaken decisions may be taken in Church courts and committees. Individual members may be seriously offended by lack of tact and wisdom on the part of others who should have known better. Parents make psychological mistakes in dealing with their own children. At times we may think we are doing our best. A year or two later it is seen perhaps that the decision we made was the worst one possible and has done harm. How confused we become in the service of Jesus Christ!

Yet Jesus was there in the days of His flesh to restrain His disciples and cover over their errors, and He is with us today. Through the miraculous power of Jesus Christ within His Church, God can use our service though it be mingled with mistakes. He can separate what is good in our influence and service from what is bad. He can counteract evil and ensure

---

[1] Matt. 17.24-27 [2] Luke 22.49-51

that there is no mistake irretrievable. He can take the mess of poisoned pottage and use it in His service.

CHRIST AND OUR INADEQUACIES

'*And there came a man from Baal-shalisha, and brought the man of God bread of the first fruits, twenty loaves of barley, and full ears of corn in the husk thereof. And he said, Give unto the people, that they may eat. And his servitor said, What, should I set this before an hundred men?*'

One day during a period of famine a farmer from the surrounding district, no doubt at great sacrifice, brought a present of food for the college of prophets. He seems to have announced confidently that he had brought a dinner of fresh loaves and barley and corn for everyone. Elisha told some of the prophets to go and help to unload it. There was some excitement among the men at the thought of a good meal. But when they saw what the man had actually brought there were cries of dismay, and Gehazi, Elisha's servant, made a sarcastic remark. Twenty loaves and a little barley to feed a whole college!

It was a ridiculous situation, but Elisha insisted that inadequate though the offer might seem, the meal was to be proceeded with. What the man had brought had to be set before the whole company. And the miracle happened. The man's sincere offering, though apparently hopeless to meet the situation, went round and much was left over.

How like we are to this man of Baal-shalisha! For the sake of Christ we bring all we can to our service in the Church and the world, but how inadequate is our effort! Our own powers and talents and resources always seem ridiculously and depressingly short of what is needed for the task God has set us. We have never enough to go round. There are those who feel so inadequate for the task that they never attempt anything for Jesus Christ. They draw back before they start, because they know they do not have the resources required.

Yet precisely at those moments when our powers fail through our inadequacy, Jesus Christ is there to save the situation from failure and ourselves from disgrace. If we would only from the start offer what we have to Him, we would find that in a multitude of ways He can somehow take it into His hands and make it sufficient for a task greater than we ever dreamed of accomplishing. Just as God made the inadequate offering ample to go round and feed the whole college, so He can today miraculously multiply our inadequate resources, if we will only start out and go on in faith.

There are two miracles of Jesus which illustrate this. One is the healing of the epileptic boy. While Jesus was on the Mount of Transfiguration a father brought his child to the disciples to cure. But they were unable to accomplish the task. They were beaten by the difficulty of it, and a partly hostile crowd gathered round. There was a disputation with the scribes who were watching their futile efforts and Jesus was discredited. It was a miserable scene of failure in the service of Christ. The power of the disciples had proved inadequate. But soon Jesus came on the scene, heard the sorry tale of failure, took the part of His disciples, and fulfilled the work they had failed to do.[1] That gives us a picture of what often happens in Christian work when our resources are inadequate. Sometimes, it is true, He allows us to face failure; nevertheless, He is at hand to step into the midst of the pathetic situation caused by our failure to vindicate His name, and to prove Himself and His Church adequate in face of the most tragic demands of human need.

And then there is of course the story of the feeding of the five thousand with the five barley loaves and the two fishes, the small offering willingly handed over to Andrew.[2] How tragic it is that people find it hard to believe that Jesus once fed five thousand with such miraculous power, when, if we had only our eyes to see what He is doing today, we would find Him repeating this miracle daily all round us.

CHRIST AND THE ACCIDENTS THAT HINDER OUR WORK

'And the sons of the prophets said unto Elisha, Behold now, the place where we dwell with thee is too strait for us. Let us go, we pray thee, unto Jordan, and take thence every man a beam, and let us make a place there, where we may dwell.'

It was an admirable scheme. Their college building was inadequate and out of date. 'Let us build a new college,' they said. Elisha agreed. They collected the materials and tools

[1] Mark 9.14-29   [2] John 6.1-14

and chose a site by the banks of the Jordan. Then a tragic accident happened. '*As one was felling a beam, the axe head fell into the water: and he cried, and said, Alas, master! for it was borrowed.*'

In those days axes were scarce and valuable. So scarce were they that the poor prophets did not possess many of their own. This particular axe had been borrowed. It was a most tragic accident. It is the kind of thing that sometimes happens in Christian work. In our perplexity we find it hard to account for such happenings. Paul himself, when his work was hindered by such experiences, put them down to Satanic powers. 'Wherefore,' he writes to the Thessalonians, 'we would have come unto you . . . again; but Satan hindered.'[1] Moreover, the infirmity or sickness with which he was constantly afflicted, and which he found a real hindrance to his work for Christ, he called not only a 'thorn in the flesh' but also a messenger of Satan to buffet me'.[2]

We are all building for God. And in the process of building the work can be spoiled not only by our own mistakes and inadequacies but also by sheer accidents that are beyond our control. Time and time again in the lives of great Christian enterprises there has come a crisis, when something we are tempted to describe as an evil fate seems to have stepped in to threaten all success. Such things are bound to happen to us if we will throw ourselves into the service of God. We must be prepared for such accidents.

Elisha acted quickly. '*And the man of God said, Where fell it? . . . And he cut down a stick, and cast it in thither; and the iron did swim. Therefore, said he, Take it up to thee. And he put out his hand, and took it.*' We can take this miracle as a sign. It is a sign that God can overcome all devilish interference in our work. It is a sign that God will allow no chance accident really to harm the work of His Kingdom. There is no such thing as chance to those who believe that all things work together for good to those that love God.[3] For Paul even the work of the Devil could be taken up by God and made to contribute to the building up of the Kingdom. Jesus' friends once suggested to Him that if He went up to Jerusalem He might meet an untimely end. 'Are there not twelve hours in

---
[1] 1 Thess. 2.18   [2] 2. Cor. 12.7   [3] Rom. 8.28

the day?' he said. 'If any man walk in the day he stumbleth not.'[1] To Jesus there is a day for our work. Twelve hours are appointed to us. If God is with us in that time, there can be no stumbling and no accidents. Therefore we must not imagine that in the course of our service of God anything can happen that might be outside the scope of His providential care.

Surely these three little miracles are messages of great encouragement to those of us who are seeking to serve God. Their message is, 'Let us not be weary in well doing: for in due season we shall reap, if we faint not.'[2] Their message is, 'Your labour is not in vain in the Lord.'[3] Our labour may seem to be in vain. It may seem to become spoilt by mistakes, shortcomings and accidents. But it is not in vain. Let us go to our work for Christ joyfully, remembering that He can turn poison into sweetness, He can turn our little offering into abundance, and He is always there to watch in the catastrophes that come upon us. He can make the lost axe-head to swim.

[1] John 11.9   [2] Gal. 6.9   [3] 1 Cor. 15.

NAAMAN

Now Naaman, captain of the host of the king of Syria, was a great man with his master, and honourable, because by him the Lord had given deliverance unto Syria: he was also a mighty man in valour, but he was a leper. And the Syrians had gone out by companies, and had brought away captive out of the land of Israel a little maid; and she waited on Naaman's wife. And she said unto her mistress, Would God my lord were with the prophet that is in Samaria! for he would recover him of his leprosy. And one went in, and told his lord, saying, Thus and thus said the maid that is of the land of Israel. And the king of Syria said, Go to, go, and I will send a letter unto the king of Israel. And he departed, and took with him ten talents of silver, and six thousand pieces of gold, and ten changes of raiment. And he brought the letter to the king of Israel, saying, Now when this letter is come unto thee, behold, I have therewith sent Naaman my servant to thee, that thou mayest recover him of his leprosy. And it came to pass, when the king of Israel had read the letter, that he rent his clothes, and said, Am I God, to kill and to make alive, that this man doth send unto me to recover a man of his leprosy? wherefore consider, I pray you, and see how he seeketh a quarrel against me. And it was so, when Elisha the man of God had heard that the king of Israel had rent his clothes, that he sent to the king, saying, Wherefore hast thou rent thy clothes? let him come now to me, and he shall know that there is a prophet in Israel. So Naaman came with his horses and with his chariot, and stood at the door of the house of Elisha. And Elisha sent a messenger unto him, saying, Go and wash in Jordan seven times, and thy flesh shall come again to thee, and thou shalt be clean. But Naaman was wroth, and went away, and said, Behold, I thought, He will surely come out to me, and stand, and call on the name of the Lord his God, and strike his hand over the place, and recover the leper. Are not Abana and Pharpar, rivers of Damascus, better than all the waters of Israel? may I not wash in them, and be clean? So he turned, and went away in a rage. And his servants came near, and spake unto him, and said, My father, if the prophet had bid thee do some great thing, wouldest thou not have done it? how much rather then, when he saith to thee, Wash, and be clean? Then went he down, and dipped himself seven times in Jordan, according to the saying of the man of God: and his flesh came again like unto the flesh of a little child, and he was clean. And he returned to the man of God, he and all his company, and came, and stood before him: and he said, Behold, now I know that there is no God in all the earth, but in Israel;

now therefore, I pray thee, take a blessing of thy servant. But he said, As the Lord liveth, before whom I stand, I will receive none. And he urged him to take it; but he refused. And Naaman said, Shall there not then, I pray thee, be given to thy servant two mules' burden of earth? for thy servant will henceforth offer neither burnt offering nor sacrifice unto other gods, but unto the Lord. In this thing the Lord pardon thy servant, that when my master goeth into the house of Rimmon to worship there, and he leaneth on my hand, and I bow myself in the house of Rimmon: when I bow down myself in the house of Rimmon, the Lord pardon thy servant in this thing. And he said unto him, Go in peace. So he departed from him a little way. But Gehazi, the servant of Elisha the man of God, said, Behold, my master hath spared Naaman this Syrian, in not receiving at his hands that which he brought: but, as the Lord liveth, I will run after him, and take somewhat of him. So Gehazi followed after Naaman. And when Naaman saw him running after him, he lighted down from the chariot to meet him, and said, Is all well? And he said, All is well. My master hath sent me, saying, Behold, even now there be come to me from mount Ephraim two young men of the sons of the prophets: give them, I pray thee, a talent of silver, and two changes of garments. And Naaman said, Be content, take two talents. And he urged him, and bound two talents of silver in two bags, with two changes of garments, and laid them upon two of his servants; and they bare them before him. And when he came to the tower, he took them from their hand, and bestowed them in the house: and he let the men go, and they departed. But he went in, and stood before his master. And Elisha said unto him, Whence comest thou, Gehazi? And he said, Thy servant went no whither. And he said unto him, Went not mine heart with thee, when the man turned again from his chariot to meet thee? Is it a time to receive money, and to receive garments, and oliveyards, and vineyards, and sheep, and oxen, and menservants, and maidservants? The leprosy therefore of Naaman shall cleave unto thee, and unto thy seed for ever. And he went out from his presence a leper as white as snow.

2 KINGS 5.1-27

NAAMAN THE CAPTAIN OF THE HOST OF THE KING OF SYRIA

This chapter introduces us to Naaman the Syrian. When we come to know him we find that he is a man intensely proud of his native country Syria. He is in a position to enjoy what is best in Syrian life, for he is an important man at the King's court. '*Naaman, captain of the host of the king of Syria, was a great man with his master, and honourable.*'

Syria was an important and colourful country to live in at

that time. Naaman can speak with great pride of Damascus with its two fine rivers Abana and Pharpar which rose fresh and cool in the mountains of Lebanon and then poured themselves out to irrigate and refresh a glorious oasis of trees and fertile country round about Damascus, creating a beautiful situation for the glittering city which shines like a white pearl in its green setting, against the dark background of the rocky desert spaces all around. It is said that when Mahomet viewed Damascus from a distant height he refused to enter it, saying that there was only one Paradise for man and he had decided not to enjoy his on earth. The description of the ample supplies of silk and silver which Naaman could take with him on his journey abroad is meant to remind us that Syria was a place where men enjoyed wealth and leisure and could pursue culture and art in a way that was not possible in many of the surrounding nations of the time. Syria could therefore offer a man of Naaman's ability a full and interesting career, money and advancement, and a sense that he belonged to a great country.

This chapter also introduces us to two men, the background of whose life contrasts vividly with that of Naaman. As we read through it we meet Elisha the prophet of Israel and Gehazi his servant. Israel was a land often at war with Syria and often defeated by the superior Syrian armies. There men had very little of the luxury and culture which Naaman enjoyed. There the rivers were sluggish and small and muddy. Famine was frequent. Even a small portion of the wealth which Naaman could afford to throw away was regarded in Israel as a fortune beyond an ordinary man's wildest dreams. Life was much narrower and more humdrum, much less exciting and changeful, for Elisha the man of God in Israel and for Gehazi his servant than for Naaman the dashing Syrian cavalier in his splendid chariot and among his fine entourage.

Naaman despised Israel. When he saw its boasted river Jordan he laughed with scorn and called it merely a trickle of water. Because he despised the country, he despised its God. Why such a country should make the claim that its religion was the only true one in the world and its God was the only living and powerful Lord, Naaman simply could not understand.

Rimmon the God of Syria had not much reality about him and worship in his temple was certainly a dull and formal routine, but it was good enough when, after all, there was so much else in Syria to make life full and interesting.

Naaman the Syrian is living in our midst today. We call him the 'man of the world'. He is an interesting and in many ways admirable type of man. He has a real zest for life. He fully enjoys the best of all this world can offer him in culture, amusement, wealth, variety, pomp and sport. But the religion of the Bible is to him something cold and unreal compared with all this. He sees little to glory in in the Cross of Christ compared with what he has in the realm of this world. He feels that the Kingdom of God is a distant and very unattractive affair compared with the kingdoms of this world.

Elisha and Gehazi the Israelites are also living in our midst today. We call them the Church people. They represent the section of modern society who are immersed so much in the life of the Church that they seem to have little time and, indeed, little concern to enjoy to the full the life of 'the world'. They may have little experience of 'the world' for they may have been brought up fairly strictly within the sphere of the Church. Between them and the 'man of the world' there is indeed as wide a difference in background and outlook as there was between Elisha the prophet of Israel and Naaman the captain of the host of the King of Syria.

From his own point of view, the 'man of the world' feels quite certain that his way of life is vastly superior to that of the man who confines most of his life to the sphere of the Church. He feels about the man of the Church what Naaman the Syrian felt as he thought about the kind of life that these poor and rather fanatical religious men lived in Israel. After all, if we are going to measure the value and worth of life by the amount of excitement and colour and beauty, amusement and adventure it offers us, then it is not really of any advantage to become a Christian. The 'man of the world' certainly believes that he is able to enjoy much more of real and colourful 'life' than the man who is devoting his time and money and talents to the service of the Church of Christ. And sometimes the man of the Church may be tempted to feel it keenly that in contrast to his worldly neighbour the service of Christ leaves him little opportunity to increase his culture and broaden his interests.

It is a mistake to suggest, as is often done, that the life lived by those who have no faith in Christ is dull and unsatisfying and lacking in zest and sweetness. Undoubtedly there are many people who have never a care for Jesus Christ and His Church who are enjoying to the full their clubs, entertainment places, social circles and affairs—and sometimes enjoying them more than some of our Church people enjoy their Church life. Moreover, when the Church tries to imitate the 'world' and provide within its organisations and fellowship what is being offered to attract and thrill and amuse men and women in the world outside, it is seldom very successful. What Israel offers when it apes Syria can never quite touch what Syria offers to its own, and certainly never appeals to the man who is Syrian in his heart of hearts.

NAAMAN THE LEPER

But one day Naaman discovered that he had to begin to seek something else besides wealth, variety, amusement and culture. Naaman discovered one day that he had leprosy and that nothing within the whole compass of life in Syria could wash a man clean when he took leprosy. If it was a great shock for Naaman in the midst of his entertaining and absorbing life in Syria to discover that he had leprosy, it was a greater shock still for him to discover that not a man in Syria—in spite of all its science and wealth and splendour and pomp—could give him any hope of a cure. Syria gave Naaman up when he became a leper. It could give him birth, feed him, educate him, tickle his fancy and amuse him. It could pipe to him while he danced and fill his life with gaiety and variety—but it could not wash him clean. Syria had done in one way far more for Naaman than the land of Israel could ever have done for any of its children—but it could not wash him clean!

The discovery that shattered Naaman's contentment with the world he was living in is a discovery that each one of us should make, either suddenly or gradually at some time of our earthly existence—and yet few of us seem to make it! It is the shattering discovery that we too are defiled, hopelessly and incurably in our whole spiritual and moral being, and that we too need cleansing of heart and mind and soul. We have to discover that we suffer from that malady, sin, which in its inner workings and effect in the heart is so like leprosy that the men of the Old Testament made the one stand for the other.

This world, with all that it can give us apart from the Christian faith, can offer us a great deal through its culture and science and philosophy. It can help us to live full, rounded and interesting lives, but it cannot wash us clean from this thing sin, which seems to stick to our souls and threatens to poison and corrupt our whole being and to lead us downward finally to destruction in spite of all the good and great and enjoyable things this world has lavished upon us.

That is why Naaman in his day had to turn his back on Syria and his face towards Israel and become a seeker in the country which before he had so much despised. In Israel they were not as clever as the Syrians. They were not so joyous and brilliant and dashing in their ways. Life was grimmer and more humdrum. But they had men in Israel who could deal with leprosy. They had faith in a living God the Creator who was also merciful and who had the power to cleanse and renew his creation.

NAAMAN THE SEEKER

The story of Naaman's search for cleansing in the land of Israel is the story of his constant and ever-deepening humiliation, until all his pride and confidence both in himself and in everything that has formed his world in Syria were completely shattered. Only then did he find himself healed of his leprosy.

First of all he had to become humble enough to listen to the wisdom of a little child rather than to that of the wise men of Syria. A little maid who had been carried captive from Israel after one of the raids made by Syrian troops happened to be the slave of Naaman's wife, and when she heard what was wrong with Naaman she went to her mistress and said, '*Would God my lord were with the prophet that is in Samaria! for he would recover him of his leprosy*'. The significant point in this part of the story is that this little Israelite child knew more about the true solution for the deepest problem of Naaman's life than all the doctors and priests and nobles of Syria put together!

'I thank thee, O Father, Lord of heaven and earth,' said Jesus once, 'because thou hast hid these things from the wise and prudent, and hast revealed them unto babes. Even so, Father: for so it seemed good in thy sight.'[1]

The 'babes', who in their simplicity can repeat to us the texts about the love of God and the saving work of Jesus Christ or the hymns they learn in Sunday School about the green hill far away

> Where the dear Lord was crucified
> Who died to save us all,

can tell us more about how to solve the deepest problem of our own lives and the deepest problems of the world's life than many of the great of this world. Perhaps that is why Jesus once set a little child in the midst of His disciples and said to them, 'Except ye be converted, and become as little children, ye shall not enter into the kingdom of heaven.'[2]

The next step in Naaman's humiliation was that he had to give up his faith in the worth of his Syrian culture and wealth and importance. Even though he had become humble enough to listen to the word of the little slave girl about the power of the prophet in Samaria, Naaman went to Israel full of pride and full of determination not to come under any real debt to the prophet of the God of this country. He determined that he would pay every penny it was worth for the healing he sought. He would take the best that Syria could offer. '*He ... took with him ten talents of silver, and six thousand pieces of gold, and ten changes of raiment.*' He was determined he would impress them with his character and stature. He would take his finest horses and chariot. He would cut a brave and fine figure. He would parade his wealth and splendour. He would take letters from the king of Syria himself. Surely all this would be enough to gain quick entrance into the palaces and temples of this backward and insignificant little province of Israel? Surely all this would gain the ear and attention of its leading religious men and ensure his speedy recovery?

He expected too that the healing virtue he sought would be found in the places where money speaks and earthly importance matters. Naturally the first place he went to was the palace of

[1] Matt. 11.25-26 [2] Matt. 18.3

the king. From his experience in Syria he reckoned that it was there that the typical priest of religion would come running at the first summons from royal authority. He expected a very dignified and worthy ceremony to be performed. He had rehearsed it in his own imagination. The prophet he imagined would come up to him and '*strike his hand over the place, and recover the leper*'.

How quickly all his false expectations were shattered! He received shock after shock to his preconceived ideas of how things should work when one dealt with the God of Israel. The prophet was not to be found at the palace and Naaman had to take his chariot and stately caravan to stand outside a humble dwelling house where they looked a most ridiculous sight. His Syrian gold and importance mattered nothing. Elisha did not even bother to come out and look at them. His letter from the king was left unread. Instead of a noble and dignified piece of ritual being performed for the benefit of his pride, all he received was a curt message, '*Go and wash in Jordan seven times*'.

He had to wash in the Jordan—when Abana and Pharphar, the rivers of Damascus, were better than all the waters of Israel! He had to do nothing hard, nothing noble, nothing costly, but merely wash and be clean! That he must come to Israel for the cleansing Syria could not give him had been a hard enough lesson for Naaman to learn at the start of his search for healing. But now to find that consistently and ruthlessly he was being subjected to an ever-deepening process of humiliation so offended him that he almost fled from Israel never to return. In anger over his wounded pride he nearly returned back to Damascus, but the thought came—how simple a thing it was, to wash and be clean. How futile to look elsewhere in his need. How much was at stake. It was the appeal of his servants that finally clinched the matter: '*If the prophet had bid thee do some great thing, wouldest thou not have done it? how much rather then, when he saith to thee, Wash, and be clean?*'

Many of us in our search for what lies at the heart of the Gospel of Christ have to go through a similar process of humiliation as we seek to grasp what Jesus Christ offers to give us. We are apt to approach Jesus Christ imagining as Naaman did when he came to Israel that there is something about us that marks us out as worth saving and worth dealing with. We like to think that even though with all our culture and moral discipline we cannot save ourselves, nevertheless, these things can take us a long way towards achieving the goal to which we hope Jesus will lift us. We want to feel that in the realm of the Christian faith culture and character matter a good deal and that God will deal with us in a manner that upholds both His dignity and our own.

The heart of the message of the Gospel is bound to be an offence to us when we listen to it with this attitude. For the Gospel is uncompromising in what it proclaims. As Elisha stood firmly by the principle that nothing that Israel could give to Naaman could be bought with the silver and gold and raiment he had brought, so the Gospel always emphasises that the gift of salvation cannot be matched with anything the world gives to men. If a man is to be saved by Jesus Christ, then neither his silver and gold, nor his culture, wisdom and learning, nor his moral character and respectability matter anything. None of the things the world values highly is of any avail to make it either more or less possible for any man to be saved. One thing and one thing alone makes it possible for a man to be saved by Jesus Christ, and that is 'The blood of Jesus Christ... cleanseth us from all sin'.[1] The Gospel offends us. It offends us as Naaman was offended by the sheer simplicity of its message. *'Wash, and be clean'* is what it says. No more than that is required, and yet we expected to be asked to do something more thrilling and adventurous! The Gospel, moreover, offends us as Naaman was offended in our expectation that God will preserve His own dignity and ours in His means of saving us, for it is to the Cross with all its crudity and horror that we are pointed as the source of our salvation, and besides this it sometimes pleases God to use the cruder and more humiliating sides of the Church's witness and proclamation rather than its dignified and cultured aspects in bringing home to us the power and meaning of the Cross of Christ.

NAAMAN THE ISRAELITE AND GEHAZI THE SYRIAN

When Naaman came up out of the water and found himself cleansed he ceased to belong any more in heart and affection

[1] 1 John 1.7

to Syria. He ceased to belong to Rimmon the god of Syria. He had seen the emptiness of worship in Syria and the inability of its life and culture to meet the needs of men. '*Now I know that there is no God in all the earth, but in Israel.*'

But he had to go back and live in Syria. He had a home and a family there. His duty was to fulfil the contracts he had undertaken there. He had to live as a Syrian in Syria. Indeed he felt that he must even go back and bow with his master in the temple of Rimmon. Yet in all this his heart would be no longer in Syria but in Israel, and his true allegiance would be to the God of Israel. As a token of this he asked Elisha to let him take back three mules' burdens of earth from Israel so that he might henceforth have a spot in Syria on which he would be able to worship and offer sacrifice to the God of Israel. He vowed henceforth to worship no other God but asked pardon if he should have to bow down with the king of Syria and his court in the now meaningless services in the temple of Rimmon.

It is at this point in the story that Gehazi, Elisha's servant suddenly revealed his true nature, and his character and attitude are sharply contrasted with those of Naaman.

Before Naaman finally said farewell he wanted to leave a present of Syrian gold and silver and silks with Elisha. '*I pray thee,*' he pleaded, '*take a blessing of thy servant.*' But Elisha was firm in his refusal. He did not want it to be imagined by anyone that the help of God of Israel could be bought for money. Moreover, the lesson of the complete independence of the grace of God from the culture of this world had to be taught to the world outside Israel without any compromise.

But Gehazi was there and he saw the proposed present which Naaman displayed before his master. His eye caught the sheen of the silk and the glitter of the gold as Naaman packed it all up and had it stowed away in the chariot. Gehazi should have been proud of Elisha's action in scorning to take what Syria could offer—especially since it reinforced the witness that was to be given in the world to the healing and free grace of the God he served. Gehazi should have been content with this, and content with his lot in Israel apart from anything that could come to him from the outside world. He had been brought up to know from his childhood that there was no other God than the God he served. He had seen with his own eyes many convincing proofs of God's power and reality.

But Gehazi was not content in Israel. He could not understand Elisha for letting pass this wonderful opportunity of enrichment from Syria. To him it was nothing more than sheer stupidity and narrow-minded principle that had kept Elisha from taking such a gift. And now Gehazi, perhaps for the first time in his life, knew where his heart was. His heart was not in Israel. He had to live and work there certainly. Indeed he had to do his job at the very centre of its religious life, but his heart was not in the service of the God of Israel. His heart was in the gold and silver and silk that he had seen Naaman pack up and throw back in his chariot as if it were mere rubbish. His heart was in the land that could produce and display all that. And having caught a glimpse of what Syria could offer he was even less content with what Israel could give him. Gehazi was maddened by the thought that Elisha had been offered a chance of having a little bit of Syria in Israel and had refused it and now Naaman was taking back a little bit of Israel to Syria!

When Elisha was not looking Gehazi ran after the chariot. He must have run with terrific speed to make up on the dashing and exultant Naaman. The energy which the love of money and the love of the 'world' can inspire in its devotees is always astonishing. He managed somehow to overtake the Syrians and he told a base and clever lie. '*My master hath sent me, saying, Behold even now there be come to me . . . two young men of the sons of the prophets: give them, I pray thee, a talent of silver, and two changes of raiment.*'

Gehazi got what he wanted, and what his heart had lusted after for many years. We must not imagine that this was a sudden downfall. It was merely the revelation of what had been in Gehazi for years. It was the revelation of the fact that for years the heart of this churchman had been more in the world outside than in his Church, and more in what the world could offer him than in what his Church could give. And yet Gehazi after his final downfall came back expecting to resume his place in the life of the Church as if nothing had happened. He went home secretly and hid his booty in a concealed place in the house and '*he went in, and stood before his master*'.

The story has a sequel that shocks us. '*And Elisha said unto him, Whence comest thou, Gehazi? And he said, Thy servant went no whither. And he said unto him, Went not mine heart with thee, when the man turned again from his chariot to meet thee?* ... *The leprosy therefore of Naaman shall cleave unto thee, and unto thy seed for ever. And he went out from his presence a leper as white as snow.*'

Here is a vivid and astonishing contrast. '*Go in peace,*' Elisha had said to Naaman and he went back to Syria. Naaman the 'man of the world' was saved from the leprosy of Syria, and he was allowed by God to go back to Syria and partake of its life and business. He was allowed even to bow down with the Syrian court in the temple of Rimmon, on one condition only. His heart must remain for ever in Israel and the three mules' burden of earth on which he sacrificed to the God of Israel in the heart of Syria must be a sign of this. He could partake almost to the full of life in Syria, but as long as he remained detached in heart and spirit and asked pardon continually for the compromise in which his life was involved he was cleansed and allowed to '*go in peace*', and was kept from any fatal contamination from his environment. Yet Gehazi the man of the Church, even though he made no journey to Syria and merely lusted after and touched a little of its silver and its silk, was smitten by the worst contamination that life in Syria could give a man. He was smitten by the leprosy that clung to Naaman. For even though Gehazi was and still remained immersed in the life of the Church, his heart was not with God but in what the world outside could give a man apart from God.

The urgent question which this contrast between these two men raises with each of us is: Where is your heart? 'Where your treasure is, there will your heart be also.'[1] God judges us finally by the true answer to this question. Where is our treasure? What do we count as our chief end, our chief gain, our main pleasure and happiness in life? Is that to be found for us in Israel or in Syria? We are not judged in the ultimate issue of things by where our job is. In this world as in Syria many men are compromised and what we do outwardly cannot always express where our heart is. Naaman had an exceedingly 'worldly' job, and even though his heart was not

[1] Matt. 6.21

in it he went through with it feeling that it had to be. Nor are we judged always by what our amusements are, though perhaps here there is more free choice to express what is in our hearts. But we are judged by where our *heart* is. That is the first and fundamental question God asks of men as He judges them.

This story warns us that we must not imagine that being immersed from Monday to Friday as well as on Sunday in the life of the Church means that our heart is in the right place. Gehazi was immersed in the life of the Church from his youth up but his heart was wrong. Elisha's word of judgment on him warns us that Gehazi will have his seed in every generation, and that the leprosy of Naaman shall cleave to them for ever. Gehazi perhaps has his seed immersed in the life of the Church today. Yet for all their Church activity and apparent devotion to its life, they are no nearer salvation than those who are enjoying to the full all they can of life that the world offers outside the Church. The leprosy of Naaman can cling to a man even though he has never been inside the door of a picture house or a gaming saloon or a dance hall. The first question that matters is, Where is your heart? And when that is settled today the other questions of conduct have a way of settling themselves.

Where is your heart? How hard it is for us to tell where. God alone knows where a man's heart is and what a man trusts in. 'The heart is deceitful above all things, and desperately wicked: who can know it? I the Lord search the heart, I try the reins.'[1] We find it hard to tell at times where our heart is. And yet there is one thing of which we can be sure. There is a river in which any man whether he be of the seed of Gehazi or the seed of Naaman can wash and be clean. 'If we say that we have no sin, we deceive ourselves, and the truth is not in us. If we confess our sins, he is faithful and just to forgive our sins, and to cleanse us from all unrighteousness.'[2] Why not wash and be clean?

[1] Jer. 17.9-10 [2] 1 John 1.8-9

SYRIA WARS AGAINST ISRAEL

Then the king of Syria warred against Israel, and took counsel with his servants, saying, In such and such a place shall be my camp. And the man of God sent unto the king of Israel, saying, Beware that thou pass not such a place; for thither the Syrians are come down. And the king of Israel sent to the place which the man of God told him and warned him of, and saved himself there, not once nor twice. Therefore the heart of the king of Syria was sore troubled for this thing; and he called his servants, and said unto them, Will ye not shew me which of us is for the king of Israel? And one of his servants said, None, my lord, O king: but Elisha, the prophet that is in Israel, telleth the king of Israel the words that thou speakest in thy bedchamber. And he said, Go and spy where he is, that I may send and fetch him. And it was told him, saying, Behold, he is in Dothan. Therefore sent he thither horses, and chariots, and a great host: and they came by night, and compassed the city about. And when the servant of the man of God was risen early, and gone forth, behold, an host compassed the city both with horses and chariots. And his servant said unto him, Alas, my master! how shall we do? And he answered, Fear not: for they that be with us are more than they that be with them. And Elisha prayed, and said, Lord, I pray thee, open his eyes, that he may see. And the Lord opened the eyes of the young man; and he saw: and, behold, the mountain was full of horses and chariots of fire round about Elisha. And when they came down to him, Elisha prayed unto the Lord, and said, Smite this people, I pray thee, with blindness. And he smote them with blindness according to the word of Elisha. And Elisha said unto them, This is not the way, neither is this the city: follow me, and I will bring you to the man whom ye seek. But he led them to Samaria. And it came to pass, when they were come into Samaria, that Elisha said, Lord, open the eyes of these men, that they may see. And the Lord opened their eyes, and they saw; and, behold, they were in the midst of Samaria. And the king of Israel said unto Elisha, when he saw them, My father, shall I smite them? shall I smite them? And he answered, Thou shalt not smite them: wouldest thou smite those whom thou hast taken captive with thy sword and with thy bow? set bread and water before them, that they may eat and drink, and go to their master. And he prepared great provision for them: and when they had eaten and drunk, he sent them away, and they went to their master. So the bands of Syria came no more into the land of Israel.

2 KINGS 6.8-23

The Folly of Fighting against God

'*The king of Syria warred against Israel and took counsel with his servants, saying, In such and such a place shall be my camp.*'
The king of Syria had deliberately started this war against his old enemy Israel. We see him holding a council of war with his staff officers to plan his campaign. He is determined to deliver a knock-out blow. He was in such a position that there was no reason why he should not be able to pull off a highly successful lightning offensive. Then it would be all over. He had the better troops, the more modern methods, and much superior equipment. He had in his high command one or two strategical geniuses such as Naaman. He had a first-class intelligence service—a fifth column of spies all over Israel. He was fortified too by the knowledge that Jehoram, the king of Israel, was a man of little determination or skill. We can almost see the king of Syria bending over the maps with his staff officers. '*In such and such a place shall be my camp,*' he says.

But the king of Syria was badly frustrated. His clever strategy all came to nothing. Time and again after the most skilful and successful moving of his troops to a vantage spot for attack, he found that when the moment to strike the blow came, the Israelites had vanished. He was thwarted in every plan he made. It was maddening to him that these people with their dull minds and inefficient military methods should out-manœuvre him at every turn. He became troubled. The only explanation that he could think of was that someone on his side was playing traitor, so he summoned a second council of war. This time the atmosphere was not quite so optimistic. Time was being lost and time was on the side of Israel. '*Therefore the heart of the king of Syria was sore troubled for this thing; and he called his servants, and said unto them, Will ye not shew me which of us is for the king of Israel?*'

The answer which someone eventually gave was far more disturbing than the discovery of a traitor in his ranks would have been. One of his servants affirmed that the Israelites had a God who knew all things, who could see through shut doors and read the secret thoughts of men's hearts; and this God had a prophet in Israel to whom He revealed what the enemies of Israel were going to do: '*Elisha, the prophet that is in Israel, telleth the king of Israel the words that thou speakest in thy bedchamber.*'

It was a disturbing discovery. Hitherto the king of Syria had thought that he was fighting simply Israel. He had thought that all he was up against was Jehoram and a contemptible army of badly equipped men. Now he discovered that he was up against the God of Israel, who had been actually fighting against him and thwarting his hope of victory. No wonder the king had felt frustrated. No wonder that he had seen his plans come to nothing. He should have at least hesitated when he heard that it was the living God he was fighting against. Naaman the captain of his host had recently brought back to Syria convincing proof of the power and reality of the God of Israel. The king should have disbanded his troops and called off the war. But instead he hardened himself.

When Henry II lost in battle one of his favourite French towns he felt so embittered that he made a vow that since God had robbed him of the town he had loved he would pay God back by robbing God of what He loved—the soul of Henry II. Such was in effect the decision of the king of Syria in face of the frustration that God had brought into his life. He challenged God to a straight fight. He planned to attack God in His headquarters and to strike a paralysing blow by capturing the prophet through whom God was working. He left nothing to chance. '*Go and spy where he is, that I may send and fetch him. And it was told him, saying, Behold, he is in Dothan. Therefore sent he thither horses, and chariots, and a great host.*'

It was a foolish plan and God answered his folly with ridicule. He made a laughing stock of the whole proud army. Without a blow being struck the magnificent Syrian host was led like a pack of blind sheep right into the power of the nation they had despised. 'He that sitteth in the heavens shall laugh: the Lord shall have them in derision.'[1]

God might have answered the Syrian king's folly in sterner ways. He answered Pharaoh with destruction when Pharaoh persisted in his obstinacy. But God's power is no less manifest in His power to ridicule than it is in His power to destroy. It is a foolish, dangerous game to keep it up against God.

Even today many of us are still in danger of committing the

[1] Ps. 2.4

folly of fighting against God. It is a danger against which we are twice explicitly warned in the New Testament. It was the folly of Saul of Tarsus before his conversion that in dedicating himself to a campaign to persecute the Church of Christ he was in reality fighting against Jesus Christ the Lord Himself. In our own case we are tempted to fight against Him by trying to push open doors that obviously God has shut, to chafe against the limitations set to our life by the law of God, to rebel with bitterness when our self-conceived plans for our own careers and our pleasures come to nothing because they have been frustrated by God's providential hand. To refuse to surrender to God when we find our life obviously limited by Him and our own plans obviously brought to nothing by His hand is the most foolish game to play in life, and it is this more than anything else that is behind the vague sense of frustration under which many people are labouring today. We are seeking to assert our frail human will against God's, and He will not yield to us. But we will not yield to Him. We cling to our plans and ambitions. Therefore things go more and more wrong with our self-made plans and we become more and more frustrated.

The first step towards attaining the cure for our sense of frustration is to realise that it is indeed God, and not merely hard circumstances or 'bad luck', that we are fighting against. That is what had to happen to Saul of Tarsus at the time of his conversion on the Damascus Road. He found himself suddenly strichen to the ground and blinded like the Syrian host at Dothan, and he realised in that moment that it was indeed against God that he had been fighting all the time. He heard the voice of Jesus saying, 'Saul, Saul, why persecutest thou me? . . . it is hard for thee to kick against the pricks.'[1] How foolish he realised then it had been for him to fight against God in Jesus Christ! But as soon as Saul acknowledged himself beaten and accepted defeat at the hands of God, he became more than a conqueror, strong in his weakness, seeing glorious things where before he had been blind, and able now to fight the good fight of faith on the side of God instead of against God. To acknowledge that we are beaten, to surrender and accept defeat at the hands of God, may be for some of us

[1] Acts 9.4-5

the start we need to make to a new life of usefulness and satisfaction such as we have never been able to experience. 'Let us not seek,' prayed Augustine, 'to bend the straight to the crooked, that is Thy will to ours, but let us seek to bend the crooked to the straight, that is our will to Thine.'

The Folly of Mistrusting God

While the war between Syria and Israel was in progress there was a crisis when Elisha's servant gave way to a foolish expression of mistrust in God. He had from all human calculations good reason for fear. When the Syrian host was sent to capture Elisha he and his master were trapped in the little town of Dothan, apparently defenceless. The hosts of the enemy surrounded the town by night and in the morning the servant of Elisha looked out and '*an host compassed the city both with horses and chariots. And his servant said unto him, Alas, my master! how shall we do?*'

He mistrusted God! He was with Elisha the man of God whom God had never deserted or failed, and he was afraid! He had seen how time and again God had frustrated the plans of these very enemies now at the gates of Dothan, and yet he was in terror! Elisha was cool and pitiful. '*Fear not,*' he said, '*for they that be with us are more than they that be with them. . . . Lord, I pray thee, open his eyes, that he may see. And the Lord opened the eyes of the young man; and he saw: and, behold the mountain was full of horses and chariots of fire round about Elisha.*' And the poor trembling servant was shown up as a foolish man. It was a different kind of folly from the folly of the king of Syria, but it was folly indeed to think that God would fail those whom He had called to stand by His side.

We are reminded of the scene on the lake when Jesus and His disciples were in the boat and a great storm arose. Jesus slept in peace. But the disciples lost their heads and their senses. They should have remembered that their boat carried Jesus Christ and that, being with Him, they were bound to be in the hands of the Heavenly Father. But they gave way to fear and they awoke Jesus saying, 'Master, carest thou not that we perish?' 'Why are ye so fearful,' He asked, 'How is it that ye have no faith?'[1]

[1] Mark 4.38-40

'*Lord, . . . open his eyes, that he may see!*'—'Why are ye so fearful?' Faith sees what is invisible. It sees behind the visible alien forces all the heavenly resources and reinforcements of love and power that are there available for all who ally themselves with the cause of God. It sees in the darkest day the light of God's glory. It sees behind the very lilies and the sparrows the Heavenly Father's promise of never-failing providence. 'If God so clothe the grass of the field, which today is, and tomorrow is cast into the oven, shall he not much more clothe you, O ye of little faith?'[1] To such faith fear is to be thought of as folly to be pitied rather than as deliberate wickedness. 'He that spared not his own Son,' says Paul, 'how shall he not with him also freely give us all things?'[2] How foolish not to believe that the love that has provided the infinitely costly gift will at the same time grudge to provide the paper and the wrappings that in comparison seem of no consequence!

The Folly of Overstepping God

The third man to show himself foolish in the presence of Elisha was Jehoram, the king of Israel. The Syrians stricken with blindness were led helpless into his hands. God in some miraculous way put his enemies into his power. Here, blind and helpless before him, were the men who had ravaged his land and sworn proud things against him. '*Shall I smite them?*' he cried to Elisha. '*Shall I smite them?*' He was thirsting for revenge. He was going to pay them back for the humiliation they had inflicted upon him and his country. Jehoram felt that God had not done enough. God had not known His business in being so lenient with His enemies. Now was the hour of vengeance! '*Shall I smite them?*' Elisha simply told him not to be foolish: '*Thou shalt not smite them: wouldest thou smite those whom thou hast taken captive with thy sword and with thy bow?*' Nor must he merely desist from vengeance: '*Set bread and water before them, that they may eat and drink, and go to their master,*' continued Elisha. God had taught them a lesson. It was not for any man to seek to improve upon God's teaching.

Shall we smite? The world is full of those who suffer because of their sin and folly. Frequently we see people fully exposed

[1] Matt. 6.30 [2] Rom. 8.32

in their sin, humiliated before God and man, shown up to have greatly wronged others or to be deeply sunk in evil. It is God who has exposed them thus and humiliated them thus, and they lie defenceless at our mercy. It is so easy for us now to smite them. We can talk and spread the story of their downfall. How often is vindictiveness practised towards defeated enemies, whether in international or in social life!

But God hates us so to take advantage of men when they are suffering humiliation under His judgment. In the Book of Zechariah God declares His displeasure with those who take advantage of His acts of judgment to satisfy their lust for personal revenge. 'I am very sore displeased with the heathen that are at ease: for I was but a little displeased, and they helped forward the affliction.'[1] They helped forward the affliction! God had afflicted Jerusalem, punished it for its sins. The surrounding nations came round and plundered it when it was down, and laughed at its weak and humiliated inhabitants. God is sore displeased with us when we take needless vengeance and smite those whom He has already smitten. We must beware of overstepping God.

The Gospel shows us a more excellent way. 'Brethren,' says Paul, 'if a man be overtaken in a fault, ye which are spiritual, restore such an one in the spirit of meekness; considering thyself, lest thou also be tempted. Bear ye one another's burdens, and so fulfil the law of Christ.'[2] 'If thine enemy hunger; feed him.'[3] 'Pray for them which dispitefully use you, and persecute you.'[4] 'Dearly beloved, avenge not yourselves, but rather give place unto wrath: for it is written, Vengeance is mine; I will repay, saith the Lord.'[5]

[1] Zech. 1.15　　　[2] Gal. 6.1-2　　　[3] Rom. 12.20
[4] Matt. 5.44　　　[5] Rom. 12.19

THE SIEGE OF SAMARIA

And it came to pass after this, that Ben-hadad king of Syria gathered all his host, and went up, and besieged Samaria. And there was a great famine in Samaria: and, behold, they besieged it, until an ass's head was sold for fourscore pieces of silver, and the fourth part of a cab of dove's dung for five pieces of silver. And as the king of Israel was passing by upon the wall, there cried a woman unto him, saying, Help, my lord, O king. And he said, If the Lord do not help thee, whence shall I help thee? out of the barnfloor, or out of the winepress? And the king said unto her, What aileth thee? And she answered, This woman said unto me, Give thy son, that we may eat him to day, and we will eat my son to morrow. So we boiled my son, and did eat him: and I said unto her on the next day, Give thy son, that we may eat him: and she hath hid her son. And it came to pass, when the king heard the words of the woman, that he rent his clothes; and he passed by upon the wall, and the people looked, and, behold, he had sackcloth within upon his flesh. Then he said, God do so and more also to me, if the head of Elisha the son of Shaphat shall stand on him this day. But Elisha sat in his house, and the elders sat with him; and the king sent a man from before him: but ere the messenger came to him, he said to the elders, See ye how this son of a murderer hath sent to take away mine head? look, when the messenger cometh, shut the door, and hold him fast at the door: is not the sound of his master's feet behind him? And while he yet talked with them, behold, the messenger came down unto him: and he said, Behold, this evil is of the Lord; what should I wait for the Lord any longer? Then Elisha said, Hear ye the word of the Lord; Thus saith the Lord, To morrow about this time shall a measure of fine flour be sold for a shekel, and two measures of barley for a shekel, in the gate of Samaria. Then a lord on whose hand the king leaned answered the man of God, and said, Behold, if the Lord would make windows in heaven, might this thing be? And he said, Behold, thou shalt see it with thine eyes, but shalt not eat thereof.

And there were four leprous men at the entering in of the gate: and they said one to another, Why sit we here until we die? If we say, We will enter into the city, then the famine is in the city, and we shall die there: and if we sit still here, we die also. Now therefore come, and let us fall unto the host of the Syrians: if they save us alive, we shall live; and if they kill us, we shall but die. And they rose up in the twilight, to go unto the camp of the Syrians: and when they come to the uttermost part of the camp of Syria, behold, there was no man there. For the Lord had made the host of the

Syrians to hear a noise of chariots, and a noise of horses, even the noise of a great host: and they said one to another, Lo, the king of Israel hath hired against us the kings of the Hittites, and the kings of the Egyptians, to come upon us. Wherefore they arose and fled in the twilight, and left their tents, and their horses, and their asses, even the camp as it was, and fled for their life. And when these lepers came to the uttermost part of the camp, they went into one tent, and did eat and drink, and carried thence silver, and gold, and raiment, and went and hid it; and came again and entered into another tent, and carried thence also, and went and hid it. Then they said one to another, We do not well: this day is a day of good tidings, and we hold our peace: if we tarry till the morning light, some mischief will come upon us: now therefore come, that we may go and tell the king's household, So they came and called unto the porter of the city: and they told them, saying, We came to the camp of the Syrians, and, behold, there was no man there, neither voice of man, but horses tied, and asses tied, and the tents as they were. And he called the porters; and they told it to the king's house within. And the king arose in the night, and said unto his servants, I will now shew you what the Syrians have done to us. They know that we be hungry; therefore are they gone out of the camp to hide themselves in the field, saying, When they come out of the city, we shall catch them alive, and get into the city. And one of his servants answered and said, Let some take, I pray thee, five of the horses that remain, which are left in the city, (behold, they are as all the multitude of Israel that are left in it: behold, I say, they are even as all the multitude of the Israelites that are consumed:) and let us send and see. They took therefore two chariot horses; and the king sent after the host of the Syrians, saying, Go and see. And they went after them unto Jordan: and, lo, all the way was full of garments and vessels, which the Syrians had cast away in their haste. And the messengers returned, and told the king. And the people went out, and spoiled the tents of the Syrians. So a measure of fine flour was sold for a shekel, and two measures of barley for a shekel, according to the word of the Lord. And the king appointed the lord on whose hand he leaned to have the charge of the gate: and the people trode upon him in the gate, and he died, as the man of God had said, who spake when the king came down to him. And it came to pass as the man of God had spoken to the king, saying, Two measures of barley for a shekel, and a measure of fine flour for a shekel, shall be to morrow about this time in the gate of Samaria: And that lord answered the man of God, and said, Now, behold, if the Lord should make windows in heaven, might such a thing be? And he said, Behold, thou shalt see it with thine eyes, but shalt not eat thereof. And so it fell out unto him: for the people trode upon him in the gate, and he died.

2 KINGS 6.24-33, 7.1-20

Human Nature?

As we read about the deeds of human vileness described in this chapter we are warned about the shameful and terrible depths of depravity to which our frail human nature can sink. '*And it came to pass . . . that Ben-hadad king of Syria gathered all his host, and went up, and besieged Samaria. And there was a great famine in Samaria: and, behold, they besieged it, until an ass's head was sold for fourscore pieces of silver, and the fourth part of a cab of dove's dung for five pieces of silver.*'

It was a time of intense human suffering within the city of Samaria. When men were besieged in cities in those days so dreadful were the consequences of surrender that they held out longer than ordinary human nature could endure. The people were crying out for food. No doubt during this siege the best that is in man came out, for men can rise to great heights of heroism and self-sacrifice in such times of human stress. But the worst in man also came out. The black marketeers and the war profiteers became important figures in public life. '*An ass's head was sold for fourscore pieces of silver, and the fourth part of a cab of dove's dung* (a measure of a certain plant that made but poor feeding stuff) *for five pieces of silver.*' The war profiteers raked in the shekels and profited heedlessly from the terrible situation that the common people were in, hoping, perhaps, that the siege would last out a day or two longer. A farmer in a certain country district of Scotland during the first World War received a high price when he sold a cow, and as he pocketed the pound notes he was heard to utter the words, 'It's been a guid wee war for me!' The local people never forgot it and quoted it against him for years after.

Moreover, under the stress of the terrible circumstances, some of the women of the nation lost all their fine feelings and in lack of natural affection descended below the level of the beast, and were not even ashamed. The king of Israel, the story tells us, met two women having a fight, and on his enquiring what was the matter, one of them cried out: '*This woman said unto me, Give thy son, that we may eat him today, and we will eat my son to morrow. So we boiled my son, and did eat him: and I said unto her on the next day, Give thy son, that we may eat him: and she hath hid her son.*'

The king tried to behave better than his people. He showed a streak of nobility, and wore sackcloth hidden under his fine robes. He was not going to live in ease and comfort while his people were undergoing such sufferings. It is a relief to see such a gleam of goodness in the midst of this dark scene. But how unstable a gleam of goodness! That day when these women revealed to him the cannibalism that was rife in the city he let go of himself: '*God do so and more also to me, if the head of Elisha the son of Shaphat shall stand on him this day.*' He let his pent-up feelings loose for a moment, and resolved that he would vent them in the murder of Elisha, the man who represented God. After all, what was the use of keeping up this game of religion any longer? '*Behold, this evil is of the Lord; what should I wait for the Lord any longer?*'

Take away the grace of God and man behaves like that. In the abnormal circumstances that visited Samaria all the moral conventions that usually keep men and women respectable disappeared. The result was that theft, murder and cannibalism were committed by those who in ordinary times were perfectly normal, decent people. Women lost their natural affections. Religion went too. Men wanted to vent their spite on God. The New Testament warns us of this. It says, 'Whosoever hateth his brother is a murderer.'[1] Of course he does not get a chance to murder him. Social convention is too strong in normal times and the law is too much feared. But if there were no police force and no civilisation and no strong social conventions of respectability and decency, then murder would come out more than it does. Jesus said, 'Whosoever looketh on a woman to lust after her hath committed adultery with her already in his heart.'[2] He does not get a chance to commit the crime. He wants to remain a respectable member of society, but Jesus warns us that the potentiality to commit the outward act is there in his heart.

This story of the siege of Samaria is a story about the human nature with which each of us is born. It is a story about the human nature that Jesus took on Him and sanctified when He was born of a woman.

'The grass withereth, the flower fadeth,' cried the prophet. By 'the grass' and 'the flower', he meant human goodness.

[1] 1 John 3.15   [2] Matt. 5.28

'Surely the people is grass.'[1] Sir Winston Churchill is quoted by Dr Whale as saying in one of his speeches, 'Certain it is that while men are gathering knowledge and power with ever-increasing and measureless speed, their virtues and their wisdom have not shown any notable improvement as the centuries have rolled on. ... Under sufficient stress—starvation, terror, warlike passion or even cold intellectual frenzy—the modern man we know so well will do the most terrible deeds and his modern woman will back him up.' We may be more civilised than they were back in the days of Elisha. That means that on the surface we are more polished, but we may ask ourselves seriously if the veneer of civilisation today lies any more thickly on us than it did on them. 'Can a woman forget her sucking child, that she should not have compassion on the son of her womb? yea, they may forget.'[2] We certainly cannot deny that what men did when they crucified Jesus Christ was a deed more terrible and more significant of the real capability of human nature for evil than even what took place during the siege of Samaria. Calvary shows up the true nature of man in his sin, and in doing so it shows up the true nature not only of the generation that crucified Jesus Christ but of our own generation too.

THE CHURCH IN THE MIDST

Samaria was not God-forsaken. Elisha the prophet was there with a Word from God: 'I will save this city.' Men were to hold out against the enemy, for relief was coming. That was the theme of Elisha's preaching. A few believed it and they gathered around Elisha, and the Word of God steadied their souls. They might easily have sunk down to the general level of depravity; they shared the same tribulation, their rations were no bigger than those of the others, the Word of God did not keep them from the common disaster. But the Word of God and the fellowship they had around the Word of God kept them steadfast in faith and they met often in fellowship in the house of Elisha. Here we have a glimpse of a Church gathered together by the Word of God in the midst of an unbelieving world.

But though they gathered apart from the world in this way

[1] Isa. 40.7-8 [2] Isa. 49.15

they did not ignore the need of the world outside, and the Word they witnessed to was a Word that influenced the whole city. This may have been a small Church but it was an influential one. This group of believing men was the main force that kept the siege going. It was because of Elisha and this Church gathered round him that Samaria had not capitulated long before. Church fellowship in this city was a living and an active and indeed a dangerous thing. Men suffered for gathering round Elisha. They proclaimed their belief so that all men knew it, and they suffered because they proclaimed their belief.

'*Elisha sat in his house, and the elders sat with him; and the king sent a man from before him: but ere the messenger came to him he said to the elders, See ye how this son of a murderer hath sent to take away mine head? look, when the messenger cometh, shut the door, and hold him fast at the door: is not the sound of his master's feet behind him?*'

This Church cannot be criticised for being timid and impractical or unrealistic in its action and outlook. Its members were ready to stand up against the world for their common rights. They were ready to protect one another in the midst of the threats that came upon them. Here we have them barring the door against the police when they came to take the minister, a scene that could be paralleled from our own Church history in Scotland and from what has happened in several European countries during recent years.

It is by the Word of God that the Church must nourish its distinctive fellowship and its distinctive life in every age. The 'world' around the Church is not outwardly so hopeless, despairing and depraved today, nor so antagonistic to the Word, as it was in those days in Samaria. There is not today the same clear-cut distinction between the light of the Word of God within the Church and the darkness of the surrounding paganism. There is much brightness outside the Church today, much hope and optimism, much Christian morality and Christian culture. In surroundings that have been blessed by centuries of Christian traditions it is difficult to see where the boundary line between the Church and the 'world' can be drawn at all. Nevertheless, in Christian Britain there are already dark shadows here and there around the borders of the Church, and when we look outward from the brightness and strength that we enjoy within those borders we can see not too far away signs that may mean that some day even the Church in Christian Britain may find itself under trial and testing, and be surrounded by a world that is much more alien and cynical and antagonistic about its message than any it has faced for generations.

However this may be, however dark or however bright the world outside the Church may appear to be, the Church as it gathers round the Word of God will find that just as Elisha was there in Samaria with the Word of promise and encouragement and hope, so Jesus Christ is in its midst today with His Word of promise and challenge that tells us of the coming deliverance of this world from the bondage of sin, death and corruption under which it is at present held. By this Word the people of God will find courage and strength to witness to those around them about the power and reality of Jesus Christ, and not to fear whatever time of testing and trial may threaten them.

But such a Church, though it is apart in this way, must nevertheless in all its thinking and in all its prayers and action be concerned not simply about itself and about its own salvation but about the future and the salvation of the world outside. Its word must be a word for the world as well as for itself. Its action must be related to the world from which it has been called apart, but in which it lives and to which it belongs.

SALVATION AND JUDGMENT

The king himself came to seek Elisha. He ran after the man whom he had sent to commit his murder. Whether he came to see if the murder had been carried out or whether he had relented and was chasing up his servant to rescue the prophet, is not clear. A few short words were spoken between prophet and king and then Elisha dropped a bombshell which delayed his execution at least a day and brought matters in the city to a climax. The Word of God came to him: '*Hear ye the word of the Lord; Thus saith the Lord, To morrow about this time shall a measure of fine flour be sold for a shekel, and two measures of barley for a shekel, in the gate of Samaria.*'

It was an almost unbelievable message. There was no word of any relieving army marching to their rescue. They had no plans made to break through the Syrian lines. Food prices had rocketed, but in the midst of all this Elisha proclaimed as the Word of God that on the very next day there would be an abundance of wheat and barley and that this would be sold at their normal prices in the gate of the city.

One of the king's stewards laughed outright and scoffed publicly at the message: '*Behold, if the Lord would make windows in heaven, might this thing be?*' Elisha replied to his scoffing with a censuring word of judgment: '*Behold, thou shalt see it with thine eyes, but shalt not eat thereof.*'

The salvation which Elisha had proclaimed came. The Syrian armies fled in the night. In the morning their camp was empty and all their equipment and stores were left as a present to the beleaguered city. God had made them hear a noise. They had thought it was an attacking army and they had panicked in a way that can be accounted for partly by the lack of discipline, partly by lack of an organised system of sentries, and partly by miracle. Salvation came to the city according to the Word of God.

The first persons to enjoy the salvation were a few poor lepers who had been complete outcasts, even worse off in their plight than the cannibals in the streets of Samaria. '*There were four leprous men at the entering in of the gate: and they said one to another, Why sit we here until we die? If we say, We will enter into the city, then the famine is in the city, and we shall die there: and if we sit still here, we die also. Now therefore come, and let us fall unto the host of the Syrians: if they save us alive; we shall live, and if they kill us, we shall but die.*' All hope had gone out of their lives and they were ready to perish. Who could be so desperate as they? And they were the first to taste the wonder of the salvation that came to the city!

They went to the Syrian camp in the dim light of the morning and found the place deserted. Silver, gold, food in abundance, silks, clothing, everything they needed and everything free, and as much as they wanted. Can we not read this as a parable of the way that salvation comes to men? The poor, the despised, the leprous, those who are most desperate, the beggars from the highways and byways, are always first to enter the Kingdom of God. The publicans and the harlots enter before the Pharisees, the Gentiles before the Jews, and everything is gloriously free and plentiful to those who have nothing to pay for it in the Kingdom of God.

The beggars behaved very naturally. They helped themselves first, and then the thought came, '*This day is a day of good tidings, and we hold our peace . . . now therefore come, that we may go and tell the king's household*'. When they were satisfied they behaved better than those of us who profess to enjoy treasures untold in Christ and a glorious free salvation but do nothing to bring others into a share of what we enjoy so freely and fully ourselves.

The only man to whom judgment came in the day of salvation was the man who had scoffed at the Word of God. Many in the city were saved that day. It was not only the Church that was saved. When Jesus comes to redeem this earth, He is not coming only for the Church. God so loved the *world* that He gave His only begotten son. Heaven will perhaps be a bigger place than some people think. The doubting king was saved even though he was slow to believe the word that was brought to him by the lepers.

But to the man who scoffed came judgment. The king had appointed as captain of the guard at the gate the very man who had scoffed at Elisha's word. Food in abundance was brought to the gate of Samaria. There was a mad rush and in the throng the scoffer was swept off his feet and killed: '*For the people trode upon him in the gate, and he died.*' The women who had eaten their children were not judged. Their sin was passed over, so great is the mercy of God. But the man who scoffed at the Word of God was visited with judgment.

God is merciful and His mercy is wonderful. It blots out the most hideous of our sins if we will accept it freely as it comes to us. But one sin is more grievous and terrible than any other—the sin of the man who scoffs at the Word of God and who deliberately laughs at the message of the Gospel of Jesus Christ.

THE DEATH OF ELISHA

Now Elisha was fallen sick of his sickness whereof he died. And Joash the king of Israel came down unto him, and wept over his face, and said, O my father, my father, the chariot of Israel, and the horsemen thereof. And Elisha said unto him, Take bow and arrows. And he took unto him bow and arrows. And he said to the king of Israel, Put thine hand upon the bow. And he put his hand upon it: and Elisha put his hands upon the king's hands. And he said, Open the window eastward. And he opened it. Then Elisha said, Shoot. And he shot. And he said, The arrow of the Lord's deliverance, and the arrow of deliverance from Syria: for thou shalt smite the Syrians in Aphek, till thou have consumed them. And he said, Take the arrows. And he took them. And he said unto the king of Israel, Smite upon the ground. And he smote thrice, and stayed. And the man of God was wroth with him, and said, Thou shouldest have smitten five or six times; then hadst thou smitten Syria till thou hadst consumed it: whereas now thou shalt smite Syria but thrice.

2 KINGS 13.14-19

'*Now Elisha was fallen sick of his sickness whereof he died.*' Elisha was dying. He knew he was dying and spoke about it. So did everyone else. The king came to discuss with him the serious problems that would face Israel after he was dead.

Today we often do our best to conceal from a mortally sick person the fact that he is dying. We seldom encourage him to face seriously his approaching death. Doctors think that this is often the wisest course. Therefore at a deathbed it is seldom possible for us to be as frank and realistic with each other as were the men of the Bible. One doubts whether we have gained anything by our refusal to speak frankly to our dear ones as death approaches them. We certainly make it difficult for the minister of the Gospel to bring to men and women the timely comfort which Christ can give them in face of death.

It is a significant fact that as he watched by the deathbed of Elisha King Joash found himself up against the most urgent and pressing challenge that he had ever had to face. And the answer he gave was decisive for the rest of his life.

A Call to Responsibility

'*And Joash the king of Israel came down unto him, and wept over his face, and said, O my father, my father, the chariot of Israel, and the horsemen thereof.*'

Joash was not sorry for Elisha, he was weeping for himself. He was unprepared for this hour. He had depended too much upon this one man whom God was now taking away from him and from the nation. He had relied so much on Elisha that he had not needed to take the initiative himself or make his own decisions. Because he had felt Elisha was equal to many chariots and horsemen he had tended to neglect preparing his army for the defence of the realm. His grief was partly due to a sense of guilt over his carelessness and neglect of his duty to his kingdom. But his grief was also due to a deep sense of personal loss and danger. Joash felt at this moment that Elisha's death meant disaster for himself and his people. How could he face the future without this great man? The thought of being left by himself at the head of the nation at this critical time in the war with Syria, without Elisha's influence and Elisha's prayerfulness, appalled him. There was no one else he could turn to for help. No wonder he came down to the deathbed and wept over the old man's face. '*O my father, my father, the chariot of Israel, and the horsemen thereof.*'

Joash dreaded facing his responsibility but this was God's call to him to face it squarely for the first time and to accept it as from God. Let him begin to face with the help of no other man now, but God only, the decisions about God and about life and about Israel that were being called for from him in his position as king.

The same call to decide for ourselves, and to decide alone before God in the face of heavy and dreadful responsibility, can and must come to each of us at some time in life. The call sometimes comes when tragedy occurs and human help and friendship are taken away from us, or when men somehow fail to understand or meet our need. 'Give us help from trouble,' cried the psalmist, 'for vain is the help of man.'[1] He means not that other men are faithless and unloving, but that life is such

[1] Ps. 60.11

that at times we get beyond the reach of the very help others might be only too ready to give us. The same call to face our real life situation and need for decision alone before God can come in the hour of our own death when we are forced to face the thought of God's judgment. We die alone. Karl Heim points out that this was one of the constant themes in the preaching of Martin Luther, who continually emphasised that in the hour of death everyone must fight his own fight, none being able to die for another; at the Last Judgment each of us must plead our cause alone before God, and none can stand beside the other.

It is especially when we are faced in the midst of this life with the problem of our sin before God, and the need to find pardon here and now for our accusing conscience, that we find ourselves in this position of absolute solitariness in our individual responsibility before God. For at that moment we each have to make a decision whether or not to commit our lives into the hands of God for His mercy, whether or not to confess our sin and forsake it. We each of us must make this decision alone. One man can help to lead another so far towards seeing that such a decision has to be made, but no man can really stand near to another as that decision is being made. We each of us must answer in complete solitariness the invitation and offer by Jesus Christ of salvation.

This does not mean that Christian fellowship has no reality. Longfellow describes us as ships that pass in the night, able to communicate one moment only by giving each other one or two distant signals, then again plunged into dark isolation and distance from each other. But when a man comes to be 'in Christ' all this isolation of mind and heart and soul is banished. 'Now therefore ye are no more strangers and foreigners, but fellow-citizens with the saints, and of the household of God.'[1] He is one with all the saints. Christ saves us from the utter solitariness of the natural man. Yet even so the entrance into this glorious new community and fellowship of the Church can be made only by a real decision of faith, taken in the solitude of a man's heart, and paradoxically even while we enjoy the glorious fellowship of the Apostles and the Church in Heaven and earth and so have no more real loneliness, we do not cease

[1] Eph. 2.19

to have solemn individual responsibility for decision in the midst of the situations we meet on earth. Our Lord in the parable of the Good Samaritan describes for us each individual man passing by himself alone the mutilated body on the roadside and each making his decision with no one else there to help or to see.

A Call to Action

'*Take bow and arrows*,' said Elisha immediately to the king. '*And he took unto him bow and arrows. And he said to the king of Israel, Put thine hand upon the bow . . . and Elisha put his hands upon the king's hands. And he said, Open the window eastward. And he opened it. Then Elisha said, Shoot: And he shot.*'

To us today this all reads like a call to action. How little time Elisha gave Joash either for tears of sorrow or for confession of his failure! Joash must face the enemy instead of looking into his desolate heart. He must cease to weep with sorrow over his loss. This is no time to give vent to personal grief. His enemies are such that he has no time for many tears. Nor must he weep for remorse over his past neglect of his opportunities. He must set to work now to repair his defences and train his armies. Preparation for action is a safer attitude than brooding over the tragedies of life. Action is a better sign of repentance than tears.

There are dangers in the advice men sometimes give to others to try to forget their sorrows and problems of conscience by immersing themselves in hard activity. For no amount of activity on our part can blot out our past or put our life right with God. We must face up to the meaning and reality and the greatness of our sin and its cost to God. We must face up to the fact that our sin has wounded God's love and provoked His judgment. We must take time to look at the Cross of Christ, and to let its meaning shatter all our self-confidence and optimism till we feel utterly unfit for any Christian action. A Christian must never get beyond this:

> O break, O break, hard heart of mine!
> Thy weak self-love and guilty pride
> His Pilate and His Judas were
> Jesus, our Lord, is crucified!

> A broken heart, a fount of tears,
> Ask, and they will not be denied:
> A broken heart love's cradle is;
> Jesus, our Lord, is crucified!

Yet if the Cross has this real meaning for us, and if we have allowed and are allowing God to create in us the broken heart and the fount of tears, and if we have listened to the Word of pardon that comes through it to us, we are bound at the same time to feel ourselves gripped with an inexpressibly strong impulse to go out and throw ourselves into Christian action, not in order to drown our consciences or forget our sorrows but in order to express our gratitude. The love of Christ that breaks our hard hearts is a love that 'constraineth us' to live not unto ourselves but unto Him who died for us and rose again.[1]

Our Lord Himself never sought merely to leave men broken in heart and weeping over their past in either repentance or remorse. He always tried to point the forgiven and repentant to some action or some service, or to some future hope and possibility that their new attitude to the past had made possible. When Peter fell at His feet with penitence in the boat after the miraculous shoal of fishes, crying, 'Depart from me; for I am a sinful man, O Lord,' He immediately said, 'Fear not; from henceforth thou shalt catch men'.[2] To the woman taken in adultery He said, 'Neither do I condemn thee; go, and sin no more'.[3] To the Church at Philadelphia He sent the unforgettable message, 'I have set before thee an open door'.[4] If we have faced the Cross and heard Christ's Word of pardon we are indeed able now to go through the open door and to 'bury the past'. It cannot be altered, no matter how many tears we shed over it, and surely it is wrong that we should allow our grief over it to be continuously so great as to make us unfit for Christian service.

Paul tells us that his policy in pressing towards the mark for the prize of the high calling of God in Jesus Christ was one of 'forgetting those things which are behind, and reaching forth'.[5] A prominent newspaper editor once said, 'The secret of editing is to know what to put in the wastepaper basket'.

[1] 2 Cor. 5.14-15   [2] Luke 5.10   [3] John 8.11
[4] Rev. 3.8   [5] Phil. 3.13

A Call to Vision

Elisha finally spent his strength in a last great effort to get Joash to see that the battle he was being called to fight was not his own battle but God's, and that if he was faithful, then in the midst of it God's hand would be upon his, giving strength to his arm and direction to his effort. He raised himself from his deathbed and as Joash took the bow to shoot through the open window '*put his hands upon the king's hands*' and shouted, in exultation, '*The arrow of the Lord's deliverance, and the arrow of deliverance from Syria: for thou shalt smite the Syrians in Aphek till thou have consumed them*'.

It was a noble effort on the part of the old man to get the young monarch to see that this responsibility facing him and before which he was tempted to despair was indeed a glorious opportunity rather than a crushing burden. It was a word and sign to assure him that God had not cast off Israel as His people and still had a great and divine purpose both for the king and for the nation if they would yield and respond to His call.

We too are tempted by sheer lack of vision to look on the responsibility we have to shoulder in life as a burden to be borne grimly and resignedly rather than as a glorious opportunity of serving God and advancing His Kingdom. We all have the battle to fight of earning our daily bread and keeping ourselves disciplined in character and daily conduct in the midst of the common task today. But it is hard to see all this as being in any way connected with some great Divine purpose. Moreover, so much of our effort seems to produce no lasting impression on our surroundings. We have the sickening feeling that in our workaday life we are not needed as individuals to express our personality in what we do, but are merely insignificant and easily replaceable units in the process of modern mass production. That makes it all the more difficult for us to feel that what we do really matters and that God is indeed with us in it all.

Jesus Christ calls us to see things differently. God when He came in Christ into human life took 'the form of a slave',[1] says the New Testament. The word 'slave' expresses exactly what untold millions of people in the world today feel themselves

[1] Phil. 2.7

at heart. They feel they are merely slaves who keep the machinery going in the midst of great economic movements and international upheavals where the ordinary individual has the power to decide nothing and matters in no way. Yet the Gospel can save such people from despair because it proclaims that Christ the Son of God is with us in our 'slavery', to lay His hands on our hands, to direct our aim, and give us strength. He became a slave in order to be with slaves. God became as nothing because He loved those who are as nothing. God links up His Eternal Spirit for ever with the meanest and most insignificant of earth's tasks. If we can see this it makes an infinite difference to the whole way we live our lives. It helps us to see that it matters that we fight the battle faithfully in the midst of the apparent obscurity and drudgery and triviality of so much we have to do, for it proclaims to us that 'Your labour is not in vain in the Lord'.[1]

Nehemiah did not know this Gospel, but even in his day he caught something of this vision. His job was to build the walls of Jerusalem, hard, dull, slow work, with grumbling workmates. But Nehemiah saw it all connected with the great purpose he believed God had for Israel His people. His enemies invited him to meet them in conference because they wanted to divert him and stop the work from going forward. But Nehemiah gave the great and memorable reply, 'I am doing a great work so that I cannot come down: why should the work cease, whilst I leave it, and come down to you'.[2]

Where Joash Failed

Joash, however, in spite of Elisha's effort and enthusiasm, could not be made to see his task in this way. He did not allow his imagination to be captured and his heart to be kindled as Elisha appealed to him to yield himself to the great destiny God had for him.

Elisha tested him. '*Take the arrows,*' he cried, '*And he took them. And he said unto the king of Israel, Smite upon the ground. And he smote thrice, and stayed. And the man of God was wrath with him, and said, Thou shouldest have smitten five or six times; then hadst thou smitten Syria till thou hadst consumed it: whereas now thou shalt smite Syria but thrice.*'

[1] 1 Cor. 15.58　　　　[2] Neh. 6.3

Joash failed in the test. As Elisha saw it this should have been for Joash a great moment of kindled emotion and wholehearted dedication under the thrill of the inspiration of the knowledge that God was with him. But Joash struck only three times and that halfheartedly. It was easy to see now that Joash had been weeping not truly for Israel and the cause of God but for himself, and that his very anxiety and trembling before the future were not about the Lord's cause but about his own plight and safety.

How many of us today fail like Joash? Jesus Christ is continually seeking from us the response of wholehearted enthusiasm for a cause the vision of which should at times thrill our hearts and make us want to express ourselves in exaggerated action and language. Time and again He treats us as Elisha treated Joash and tries to get our hearts to burn within us as He gives us His call today. Time and again He tries to make us feel that His hands are on our hands as He sends us out to fight for Him and work for Him. How thrilled He was when He saw wholehearted enthusiasm—as when Mary broke her box of precious ointment over Him in apparent waste in the house at Bethany,[1] or when Peter in his moment of vision and daring cried out from the boat, 'Lord, if it be thou, bid me come unto thee on the water.'[2] The actions of both Mary and Peter could be criticised as wasteful and foolhardy. But Jesus was thrilled by both.

The cure for all our shameful and self-centred halfheartedness in the Church today is possible if we realise that God never loses His enthusiasm for His Gospel and His cause. His fire never wanes. He never slackens or grows weary of His purposes. Because of this He is always ready to kindle our cold hearts with new warmth and vision. Moses in his youth had been so full of zeal for the deliverance of Israel from Egypt that he overstepped the bounds of wisdom and killed an Egyptian. Then followed many years in Midian when he lost all vision and hope of ever doing anything to fulfil what had once been a burning purpose in his heart. But then one day he saw a bush burning with an unquenchable fire.[3] When he heard God speak he knew what the vision meant. God's heart still burned with undiminished love for His people even though

[1] Matt. 26.7   [2] Matt. 14.28   [3] Exod. 3

the flame had gone out in Moses' heart. God had in no way lost His zeal that His people should go free. And gradually at first and ever and again in his long, trying life as leader of the people, Moses knew a source to which he could turn to have vision of the glory of his task renewed and his heart made again to burn.

www.ingramcontent.com/pod-product-compliance
Lightning Source LLC
Chambersburg PA
CBHW070918180426
43192CB00038B/1757